P9-CEV-649

DATE DUE

1486.

Bible Study

HIS NAME IS WONDERFUL

BIBLE STUDY GUIDE

From the Bible-teaching ministry of

Charles R. Swindoll

INSIGHT FOR LIVING

Chuck graduated in 1963 from Dallas Theological Seminary, where he now serves as the school's fourth president, helping to prepare a new generation of men and women for the ministry. Chuck has served in pastorates in three states: Massachusetts, Texas, and California, including almost twenty-three years at the First Evangelical Free Church in Fullerton, California. His sermon messages have been aired over radio since 1979 as the *Insight for Living* broadcast. A best-selling author, Chuck has written numerous books and booklets on many subjects.

Based on the outlines and transcripts of Chuck's sermons, the study guide text is coauthored by Lee Hough, a graduate of the University of Texas at Arlington and Dallas Theological Seminary. He also wrote the Living Insights sections.

Editor in Chief:
Cynthia Swindoll

Senior Editor:
Lee Hough

Assistant Editor:
Wendy Peterson

Copy Editors:
Deborah Gibbs
Glenda Schlahta

Production Artist:
Cindy Ford

Typographer:
Bob Haskins

Director, Communications Division:
Deedee Snyder

Production Coordinator:
Susan Nelson

Production Assistant:
Ellen Galey

Assistant Print Production Manager:
John Norton

Unless otherwise identified, all Scripture references are from the New American Standard Bible, © The Lockman Foundation 1960, 1962, 1963, 1968, 1971, 1972, 1973, 1975, 1977. Used by permission. Scripture taken from the Holy Bible, New International Version © 1973, 1978, 1984 International Bible Society, used by permission of Zondervan Bible Publishers [NIV]. The other translation cited is the *King James Version* of the Bible [KJV].

An effort has been made to locate sources and obtain permission where necessary for the quotations used in this book. In the event of any unintentional omission, a modification will gladly be incorporated in future printings.

ISBN 1-57972-073-0
COVER DESIGN: Gary V. Lett
COVER PHOTOGRAPH: Jack Fritze, Neophoto
BACKGROUND HYMN: "His Name Is Wonderful" by Audrey Mieir. © 1959, renewed 1987 by Manna Music, Inc. All rights reserved. Used by permission. Taken from *Hymns for the Family of God* (Nashville, Tenn.: Paragon Associates, 1976).
Printed in the United States of America

CONTENTS

---

*This message was not a part of the original series but is compatible with it.

INTRODUCTION

The age-old question, "What's in a name?" deserves an intelligent answer, especially when it is asked about Jesus Christ. I have been thrilled with this new study! While examining one name after another, a whole world of unexpected and fresh information about our Lord has opened up to me.

We shall learn much: the meaning of His various titles, the significance of certain symbolic names, some background material on several intriguing terms related to His names, and as always, the practical and devotional benefits of understanding those identifying designations.

You may think you know Him well . . . but after these eye-opening discoveries, you will gain a whole new perspective on your Savior as well as a new appreciation for the most unique person who ever cast a shadow upon this earth. Best of all, our worship and adoration of Him will be enhanced as our understanding of His names is enlarged.

Chuck Swindoll

Chuck Swindoll

PUTTING TRUTH INTO ACTION

Knowledge apart from application falls short of God's desire for His children. He wants us to apply what we learn so that we will change and grow. This study guide was prepared with these goals in mind. As you go through the following pages, we hope your desire to discover biblical truth will grow as your understanding of God's Word increases, and that you will be encouraged to apply what you've learned.

To assist you in your study, we've included a section called **Living Insights** at the end of each lesson. These exercises will challenge you to study further and to think of specific ways to put your discoveries into action.

There are many ways to use this guide—in personal devotions, group studies, discussions with friends and family, and Sunday school classes. And, of course, it's an ideal study aid when you're listening to its corresponding "Insight for Living" radio series.

To benefit most from this study guide, we would encourage you to consider it a spiritual journal. That's why we've included space in the **Living Insights** for recording your thoughts and discoveries. We hope you'll return to those sections often for review and encouragement as you continue to grow in your walk with Christ.

Lee Hough
Coauthor of Text
Author of Living Insights

His Name Is Wonderful

Chapter 1

WE CALL HIM LORD

Selected Scriptures

T he spectacular carvings were veiled in darkness."[1] That's what
author Elmer Towns disappointedly discovered late one evening on a visit to the Mount Rushmore National Monument in
South Dakota. The floodlights that illuminated the colossal faces
of Washington, Jefferson, Lincoln, and Roosevelt had been turned
off just minutes before he arrived. And, "as a result of an imminent
storm," he recalled, "there wasn't even any moonlight."[2]

> But what I thought was a barrier became a bless-
> ing. Flashes of lightning accompanied the thunder-
> storm, and with each flash I got a quick glance at
> the great sculptures. I had certain preconceived im-
> ages in mind from photographs, and I strained to
> compare each statue with the likeness in my mind's
> eye. The more I watched, the more I realized that I
> was appreciating their magnificence and grandeur
> even more than I would have if the storm had not
> forced me to view them more intensely.
>
> In the same way, we struggle to understand God.
> We know He is there, but in the darkness of this
> life, we cannot see Him. Then come flashes of light
> that reveal Him—the creation . . . the miracles
> . . . the Ten Commandments . . . His presence
> in our conscience.
>
> But there is another flash of illumination that is
> often overlooked. We can come to know God through

---

1. Elmer L. Towns, *My Father's Names* (Ventura, Calif.: Regal Books, 1991), p. 12.

2. Towns, *My Father's Names*, p. 12.

1

His names. The many descriptive titles and names given in Scripture are like lightning flashes in a summer night, revealing His nature and works.[3]

His Name Is Wonderful is a series of lightning flashes revealing the nature and work of God's Son through His names. As we gaze intently at His true majesty and grandeur through twelve illuminating chapters, it is our prayer that each will leave you with a greater sense of awe, worship, and understanding for the One whose name is above all names—Jesus.

Significant Facts about Names

To enhance our ability to understand the flashes of names we're about to study, let's first consider some significant facts about biblical names.

Names in General

Since the beginning of time, names and titles have been important to God. From the very first paragraph of the book of beginnings, Genesis, we see Him naming His creation as it was brought forth.

> Then God said, "Let there be light"; and there was light. And God saw that the light was good; and God separated the light from the darkness. And God called the light day, and the darkness He called night. And there was evening and there was morning, one day. (Gen. 1:3–5)

On the second day, He created an expanse and christened it *heaven* (vv. 6–8). On the third day, He named the dry land *earth* and the gathering waters *seas* (vv. 9–10). And sometime after the creation of man on the sixth day, God placed Adam in the Garden of Eden and immediately put him to work naming all the animals (2:19).

Another significant fact about names is that they often convey something related to a person's birth. Take Isaac, for example. When God told Abraham, who was then ninety-nine years old, that he would have another son, the wrinkled patriarch literally fell on his face laughing. God then immediately told this chuckling skeptic that the name of his special child would be Isaac, which in Hebrew means "laughter" (17:17, 19).

---

3. Towns, *My Father's Names*, pp. 12–13.

When Pharaoh's daughter took a three-month-old baby in a basket from among the reeds of the Nile, she named him Moses, which in Hebrew means "drawn out" (Exod. 2:5, 10). And there are similar stories behind the names of Jacob, Jabez, and many others throughout history.

Names can also reveal other aspects about an individual. For example,

> it can very often happen that a name given to a man can be a one-word summary of what he has done and of what he is. . . . So the impact of Alexander on the world is summed up in his title Alexander the Great; the relationship of William to England is summed up in his title William the Conqueror. . . . The function of John in history is summed up in his title John the Baptizer; the politics and the character of Simon are contained in his title Simon the Zealot.[4]

All of this is especially true concerning Mary's Son, Jesus.

Jesus' Names

Seven hundred years before the birth of the Savior, God not only predicted His Son would come from a virgin, but He also gave Him a name.

> "Therefore the Lord Himself will give you a sign:
> Behold, a virgin will be with child and bear a son,
> and she will call His name Immanuel." (Isa. 7:14)

Immanuel literally means "God with us," telling about the incarnate nature and presence of Jesus (see Matt. 1:23). Isaiah also penned another prophecy containing names that reveal more of the nature and work of the Messiah.

> For a child will be born to us, a son will be given
>   to us;
> And the government will rest on His shoulders;
> And His name will be called Wonderful
>   Counselor, Mighty God,
> Eternal Father, Prince of Peace. (9:6)

---

4. William Barclay, *Jesus as They Saw Him* (1962; reprint, Grand Rapids, Mich.: William B. Eerdmans Publishing Co., 1980), p. 9.

We come to the fulfillment of Isaiah's prophecy, the announcement of the conception of the One named Immanuel, in Matthew 1:18–25 and Luke 1:26–28, 31–35. Even then, in the proclamation of the pregnancy, Mary and Joseph were given more names for their new son, such as Jesus, which means "Savior," and Son of the Most High, Son of God, and again, Immanuel.

And during Jesus' three years of public ministry as an adult, as people got to know Him better, they'd often begin to alter what they called Him. One classic example of this is found in John 9, where Jesus healed a blind man. At first, when the crowds questioned the beggar regarding who had healed him, he simply said, "The man who is called Jesus" (v. 11a). Later, however, when the Pharisees interrogated him about Jesus, his view had changed; and he called Him by a more important title.

> They said therefore to the blind man again, "What
> do you say about Him, since He opened your eyes?"
> And he said, "He is a prophet." (v. 17)

Finally, after the Pharisees had thrown him out of the temple (v. 34), this same man encountered Christ again, believed in Him as the Son of Man, called Him his Lord, and worshiped Him (vv. 35–38). His spiritual blindness was completely healed as his understanding of Jesus progressed from seeing Him as only a man, to seeing Him as a prophet, then as the Son of Man, and finally as the Lord!

His Name Is *Lord*

Nowadays, by far the most common title used for Jesus after His resurrection is Lord. And it is also the most important theologically. The growth of its usage and theological importance, however, was gradual.

Its Usage in Scripture

As you look back, the first gospel writer, Mark, only used the name Lord a couple of times in the same divine sense as did the man healed of blindness. Matthew mentions it a few times more than Mark; it occurs about seventeen times in Luke, and even more than that in John.

But when you get to the Epistles, Paul alone refers to Jesus as Lord more than two hundred times! Occasionally, he uses this title as many as twelve to thirteen times in a single chapter. Perhaps one of the most significant passages where Paul mentions this name is Philippians 2:5–1. In this brief but glorious section of Scripture, we move from heaven itself to the Cross and back again in a crescendo of praise that highlights His wonderful name.

> Have this attitude in yourselves which was also in Christ Jesus, who, although He existed in the form of God, did not regard equality with God a thing to be grasped, but emptied Himself, taking the form of a bondservant, and being made in the likeness of men. And being found in appearance as a man, He humbled Himself by becoming obedient to the point of death, even death on a cross. Therefore also God highly exalted Him, and bestowed on Him the name which is above every name, that at the name of Jesus every knee should bow, of those who are in heaven, and on earth, and under the earth, and that every tongue should confess that Jesus Christ is Lord, to the glory of God the Father.

All of us, every human being who has ever lived, both the saved and the unsaved, will one day confess this one name God bestowed on Jesus . . . and with that confession enter into either eternal joy or endless agony.

Meaning of the Term

The Greek term for Lord, *kurios*, was already being widely used before the early church adopted it. Let's take a look through the eyes of a learned historian to see the rich meaning behind this noble term.

> The first thing that strikes us when we study this word in detail is the *atmosphere of authority* which it carries with it. That authority operates in a variety of spheres.
> (i) It is the word of *domestic* authority. It describes the authority of the father of the family. . . .
> (ii) It is the regular word for a *master* as *opposed to a slave.*
> (iii) It is the regular word to describe the *undisputed owner* of any property.
> (iv) Kurios very commonly describes the person who has *authority to make decisions.* It describes the

commander who has the right to make military decisions. . . . It describes the magistrate who has the *legal* authority to pass sentence of death. . . .

(v) It can express *moral* authority. . . . Aristotle, for instance, uses it to describe the man who has the strength of character . . . never to allow himself to become intoxicated. . . .

. . . *Kurios* was the normal word of courtesy and respect, used in addressing an elder or a superior or some one held in affection. It was used in the same way as the English "Sir," the French "Monsieur," and the German "Herr." . . .

. . . It can be a conventional courtesy; it can be the address of a child to a parent, of a scholar to a teacher, of a servant to a master, of a slave to an owner, of a subject to his emperor, of a worshipper to his god. *Kurios* is a word whose meaning can be entered into at a wide variety of levels.[5]

Theologically, no other word is like *Lord* when it is used in the sense of imperial, sovereign authority. And there can be little doubt that when the early church ascribed this title to Jesus, to them it signified One who had the right to rule over them.

Reasons for Its Importance

No other title turns the controls over to Jesus like *kurios* does. To call Him by that name means that He alone is our authority above any other. And this was what put the early church on a collision course with the Roman empire. Commentator William Barclay explains:

Once a year a man had to come and burn a pinch of incense to the godhead of the Emperor and to say: "Caesar is Lord." That was a test of his loyalty as a citizen of the Empire; and, having done that, he could go away and worship any kind of god he liked; but that affirmation of faith in Caesar he must make. This is precisely what the Christians would not do. They would not take the name of *kurios* and give it to anyone else in earth or in heaven. For

5. Barclay, *Jesus as They Saw Him*, pp. 409–10, 414.

them Jesus was Lord, and nothing would make them say, "Caesar is Lord." And so they chose to die for their faith, and they died in the agonies of the cross, the flames, the arena, the rack. *Kurios* was the one-word creed for which the Christians were ready to lay down their lives.[6]

Kurios still is a powerful one-word creed. One that we should never take lightly. Jesus certainly doesn't.

When We Call Him *Lord* . . .

In conclusion, here is a simple A-B-C-D arrangement to help you remember the things we've learned the next time you call Jesus Lord.

When we call Him Lord . . .

A: We *affirm* our allegiance.
B: We *bow* to Christ's authority.
C: We *commit* to Him all we are, have, and hope to be.
D: We *dethrone* our own will and way.

———————◆———————

Our Father,

There is no more epochal, more important moment of the day than now, when we say down deep in our hearts where no one can see, "I acknowledge You, Christ, as Lord—my Lord. I affirm my allegiance. I bow to Your authority. I commit all I am and have and hope to be. I dethrone my will and my way, enthroning You and You alone as Lord."

Father, help us as we progressively release to You the things we have held onto, in fact, clutched. Teach us how to let go and dethrone our own will. Stay near us, encourage and comfort us, and quiet our fears. Reassure us that with You all is safe.

We thank You for the names of our Savior. We thank You this moment for the name Lord. And we acknowledge Him as that through Christ Jesus. Amen.

———

6. Barclay, *Jesus as They Saw Him*, pp. 419–20.

Lordship means ownership. The apostle Paul explained it this way:

> And He died for all, that they who live should no longer live for themselves, but for Him who died and rose again on their behalf. (2 Cor. 5:15)

Who are you living for? Who's in control? Juan Carlos Ortiz, in his book *Call to Discipleship,* poignantly brings home the truth of what it means to call Jesus Lord.

> When a man finds Jesus, . . . [he] marvels at such a pearl and says, "I want this pearl. How much does it cost?"
>
> The seller says, " . . . It costs everything you have—no more, no less—so anybody can buy it."
>
> "I'll buy it."
>
> "What do you have? Let's write it down."
>
> "I have $10,000 in the bank."
>
> "Good, $10,000. What else?"
>
> "I have nothing more. That's all I have." . . .
>
> "Where do you live?"
>
> "I live in my house."
>
> "The house too." . . .
>
> "Do you mean that I must live in my car, then?"
>
> "Have you a car?"
>
> "I have two."
>
> "Both become mine. Both cars. What else?" . . .
>
> "I have nothing else."
>
> "Are you alone in the world?"
>
> "No, I have a wife, two children. . . ."
>
> "Your wife and your children too."
>
> "Too?"
>
> "Yes, everything you have. What else?"
>
> "I have nothing else, I am left alone now."
>
> "Oh, you too. Everything. Everything becomes mine: wife, children, house, garage, cars, money, clothing, everything. And you too. Now you can use all those things here but don't forget they are mine, as you are. When I need any of the things

you are using you must give them to me because now
I am the owner."[7]

Is there a particular possession, attitude, relationship, or ability
that you are refusing to place under His authority? Take some time
to think this through, and use the space provided to write down
any areas you might be withholding from Him.

_____   _____

_____   _____

_____   _____

_____   _____

Now present these things to the Lord and commit them individually to His ownership. As you do, don't forget to submit the one
thing that is more important to Him than any of your possessions
or abilities—*you!*

 L̲iving I̲nsights _____ STUDY TWO

O magnify the Lord with me,
And let us exalt His name together.
(Ps. 34:3)

The goal of this study guide is not simply to gain information
but to increase our intimacy with Jesus. So as you work through
each chapter, the second Living Insight will be an invitation to
worship. With whatever flash of illumination each name brings, let
it prompt you to give praise and thanksgiving to Him. Name the
names of Jesus; gaze at them; memorize the outline of His character
that they reveal. Be full of awe, because, as Thomas Carlyle once
said, "Worship is transcendent wonder."[8]

As you finish praying, keep a journal of the things for which
you praised Him. Space will be provided in each chapter for your
reflections.

7. Juan Carlos Ortiz, as told to Jamie Buckingham, *Call to Discipleship* (Plainfield, N.J.:
Logos International, 1975), pp. 42–43.

8. Thomas Carlyle, as quoted in *The Oxford Dictionary of Quotations*, 3d ed. (1979; reprint,
Oxford, England: Oxford University Press, 1980), p. 131.

Begin now by focusing on *kurios*, Lord. Be silent for a time; meditate on what you've learned; ask yourself what you've seen. Pray for the Holy Spirit to open the eyes of your heart to understand and appreciate what this name discloses about Jesus.

Journal

_____

_____

_____

_____

_____

_____

_____

_____

_____

_____

_____

_____

_____

_____

_____

_____

_____

Chapter 2

HE IS "KING OF KINGS, LORD OF LORDS"

Selected Scriptures

Had we been there when Jesus was born, we probably wouldn't have believed that this tiny, bawling baby with a feeding trough for a crib was the Lord of Lords.

Had we seen Him as a boy playing around his father's carpentry shop, we wouldn't have stopped and said, "Yes, no doubt about it, Joseph, He's the supreme Ruler of the universe."

Had we met Him on His way to the Jordan River to be baptized, it's doubtful any of us would have thought this common tradesman held an imperial position as a member of the Trinity.

Who would've ever guessed that framed within such humble, human flesh was the everlasting, sovereign, and divine Ruler over all? But indeed He was, and is, as we shall see today in our study of His wonderful name—King of Kings and Lord of Lords.

Places Where This Name Occurs

To begin, let's trace the lineage of His title back to its Old Testament roots. The earliest reference is found in Deuteronomy 10:17, where Moses assigned a similar title to the Lord Jehovah.

> "For the Lord your God is the God of gods and the
> Lord of lords, the great, the mighty, and the awesome
> God who does not show partiality, nor take a bribe."

This same title is poetically ascribed to God the Father again in Psalm 136:1–4.

> Give thanks to the Lord, for He is good;
> For His lovingkindness is everlasting.
> Give thanks to the God of gods,
> For His lovingkindness is everlasting.
> Give thanks to the Lord of lords,
> For His lovingkindness is everlasting.
> To Him who alone does great wonders,
> For His lovingkindness is everlasting.

Though the title itself is not named, the substance of it is revealed in the confession King Nebuchadnezzar made at the conclusion of God's judgment upon his life in Daniel 4.

> "But at the end of that period I, Nebuchadnezzar, raised my eyes toward heaven, and my reason re-turned to me, and I blessed the Most High and praised and honored Him who lives forever;
> For His dominion is an everlasting dominion,
> And His kingdom endures from generation to generation." (v. 34)

Crossing over to the New Testament, we find that the apostle Paul specifically names God as the King of Kings and Lord of Lords in one of the most magnificent doxologies found in all of Scripture.

> I charge you in the presence of God, who gives life to all things, and of Christ Jesus, who testified the good confession before Pontius Pilate, that you keep the commandment without stain or reproach until the appearing of our Lord Jesus Christ, which He will bring about at the proper time—He who is the blessed and only Sovereign, the King of kings and Lord of lords; who alone possesses immortality and dwells in unapproachable light; whom no man has seen or can see. To Him be honor and eternal dominion! Amen. (1 Tim. 6:13–16)

And in the final book of the New Testament, God Himself leads the apostle John to apply this unique title to Jesus not once, but twice! First, it is used in a *prediction* of a final great battle:

> "These will wage war against the Lamb, and the Lamb will overcome them, because He is Lord of lords and King of kings, and those who are with Him are the called and chosen and faithful." (Rev. 17:14)

And second, it appears in a *description* of that great battle re-corded in chapter 19.

> And I saw heaven opened; and behold, a white horse, and He who sat upon it is called Faithful and True; and in righteousness He judges and wages war. And His eyes are a flame of fire, and upon His head are many diadems; and He has a name written upon

Him which no one knows except Himself. And He is clothed with a robe dipped in blood; and His name is called The Word of God. And the armies which are in heaven, clothed in fine linen, white and clean, were following Him on white horses. And from His mouth comes a sharp sword, so that with it He may smite the nations; and He will rule them with a rod of iron; and He treads the wine press of the fierce wrath of God, the Almighty. And on His robe and on His thigh He has a name written, "KING OF KINGS, AND LORD OF LORDS." (vv. 11–16)

A Careful Analysis of the Title

What exactly does this name communicate about Jesus? Simply put, it means He is over and above all who would call themselves kings or lords. In his book *Prophecy's Last Word*, Frederick Tatford defined it this way:

> He is the absolute Sovereign and supreme Ruler. All other kings, governors, and potentates are subservient to Him. He is the universal Sovereign and all authority has been committed to Him.[1]

We can glean at least four important facts about Jesus from this title. First, He has no equal. When we turn to Him, there is none greater or higher. Second, He has never been and never will be outranked, overthrown, or undermined. His reign and authority are secure. No one will ever suddenly appear who has greater power. Third, He knows no limitation, experiences no frustration, and faces no threats. Jesus never ends a day with a discontented sigh. There is no barrier He cannot overcome. And fourth, He remains absolutely invincible.

Webster defines *invincible* as "incapable of being conquered, overcome, or subdued."[2] That's why Moses could say, "Do not fear!" when the Egyptians cornered the Israelites at the Red Sea (Exod. 14:13). That's why David had the confidence to tell Goliath, "The battle is the Lord's and He will give you into our hands" (1 Sam. 17:47).

---

1. Frederick A. Tatford, *Prophecy's Last Word: An Exposition of the Revelation* (London, England: Pickering and Inglis, 1947), p. 216.

2. *Webster's Ninth New Collegiate Dictionary*, see "invincible."

For both knew that no individual, army, or power is greater than the King of Kings and Lord of Lords.

Why Is It Necessary to Acknowledge This Name?

Many reasons could be given for acknowledging Jesus as the King of Kings and Lord of Lords, but three in particular stand out. One is that we are by nature proud, self-centered people and need to be reminded of who is in charge. When we acknowledge that He is King and Lord, we dethrone ourselves and enthrone Him.

Another reason is that we are weak and need the assurance that He is absolutely reliable. Nothing we experience surprises Him. The King of Kings and Lord of Lords will never answer our prayers with, "Er, uh, I'd sure like to help, but I just don't know what to do." He is always in control and always accomplishes His will.

Last, acknowledging His name is necessary because we face an insidious enemy—we need to remember that Christ can handle any adversary. As the apostle John reminds us, "Greater is He who is in you than he who is in the world" (1 John 4:4).

Conclusion

Had we been there when the Magi asked, "Where is He who has been born King of the Jews?" (Matt. 2:2), probably none of us would have had a clue.

Had we witnessed Jesus dying on a cross, it's not likely that many of us would have believed the placard above His bloodied head: "THIS IS JESUS THE KING OF THE JEWS" (27:37).

Who would have ever guessed that it was precisely because He was the King of Kings and Lord of Lords that He chose to let us crucify Him, allowing His priceless blood to pay the debt of our sin?

Truly, only He who conquered sin and death through such a sacrifice is worthy of the title King of Kings and Lord of Lords.

Our Father,

We thank You for Christ, who loved us and gave Himself for us. We acknowledge His authority over us and His right to reign as King over all kings and Lord above all lords. We commit to Him all the struggles of our lives—our own inadequacies, faithlessness, weaknesses,

*rebellion, wrongs, and fears. And we count on You to
hold us near and dear to Yourself, to be to us all that
You have promised, and to fulfill every word of Yours to
the last "jot and tittle" because You are God and because
we worship Your Son, Christ. In His holy, sovereign,
faithful, and true Name we pray. Amen.*

Living Insights

In our lesson, we listed four important implications of the title
King of Kings and Lord of Lords. Take some time now to meditate
on this name and see what insights you can discover for yourself.
Set aside some additional time throughout the day to ponder what
it reveals about Jesus, and use the space provided to record your
thoughts.

Your Insights

1. _____

2. _____

3. _____

4. _____

5. _____

We also listed three reasons why it's crucial to acknowledge His
name. Can you think of more? Use the following space to write
down, not just reasons for everyone, but more importantly, the
specific reasons *you* feel it is necessary to acknowledge Christ as
your King of Kings and Lord of Lords.

Acknowledging His Name

1. _____

2. _____

3. _____

4. _____

5. _____

When you hear the name King of Kings and Lord of Lords, what images come to your mind? A king on a majestic throne? A mighty warrior slashing down enemies with a glistening sword? The powerful fingers of creation sweeping colors across an evening sky or spilling torrents of water down a magnificent fall?

Close your eyes and let your mind conjure up pictures of your Sovereign Lord. You may want to focus on some words related to His Name to give you some ideas; for example, *reign, throne, power,* and so forth. As the images of Jesus' lordship come to mind, write brief descriptions of them below, using each one to prompt you to worship.

_____   _____

_____   _____

_____   _____

_____   _____

Journal

_____

_____

_____

_____

_____

_____

_____

_____

_____

_____

Chapter 3
THE MEANING OF MESSIAH
Selected Scriptures

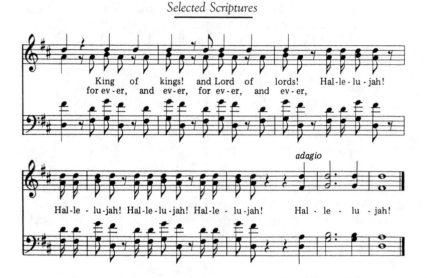

King of kings! and Lord of lords! Hal-le-lu-jah!
for ev-er, and ev-er, for ev-er, and ev-er,

adagio

Hal-le - lu-jah! Hal-le-lu-jah! Hal-le - lu-jah!   Hal - le - lu - jah!

In his magnificent coach, drawn by four plumed horses, Charles Jennens would ride to town from his country seat, an impressive and well-known figure. And on Saturday, August 22, 1741, he brought a scrapbook with him to Handel's small study. "Here," he said, "is a collection called *The Messiah*. Can you make an entertainment out of it?"

As soon as Jennens had left, the Master started reading the text he had received. The words, Handel noticed, were all taken from the Scriptures; but in arranging the quotations, the Master felt, Jennens had outdone himself. The words seemed to sing by themselves.

Handel started writing at once. He wrote so fast that the ink had scarcely dried on one page before he started another. The score was covered with splotches, but the Master did not notice them. He forgot the whole world around him.

"Whether I was in my body or out of my body as I wrote *The Messiah,*" Handel said later, "I know not." For twenty-four days he remained in the little front room on the first floor of his house near Hanover Square in London, setting down thousands of notes to Jennens' biblical excerpts. At regular intervals Handel's servant brought him food, but the Master left it untouched. Sometimes the servant stood in silent wonder as the Master's tears fell on a page and mingled with the ink while he penned his notes. And once the servant found the Master sobbing with emotion. He had just finished the "Hallelujah Chorus."

"I thought I saw all Heaven before me," Handel told his choir boys, "and the great God himself!"[1]

Does a Christmas season ever pass that isn't bedecked with the magnificent melody of Handel's masterpiece? Crescendoing in churches and concert halls, the glorious harmony of "hallelujahs" rings forth from enthusiastic carolers everywhere. Yet, oddly enough, if you were to ask most people what the title *Messiah* actually means, they wouldn't have a clue. Surprised?

They Called Him *Messiah*

You might be even more surprised to know that the name Messiah occurs only four times in all of Scripture, twice in the Old Testament and twice in the New.

Old Testament

The first two appearances are found in back-to-back verses recorded in Daniel 9.

> "So you are to know and discern that from the issuing of a decree to restore and rebuild Jerusalem until *Messiah* the Prince there will be seven weeks and sixty-two weeks; it will be built again, with plaza and moat, even in times of distress. Then after the sixty-two weeks the *Messiah* will be cut off and have nothing, and the people of the prince who is to come will destroy the city and the sanctuary. And

---

1. Hertha Pauli, *Handel and the Messiah Story* (New York, N.Y.: Meredith Press, 1968), pp. 49, 51.

its end will come with a flood; even to the end there will be war; desolations are determined." (vv. 25–26, emphasis added)

From this mysterious Old Testament foreshadowing of the Messiah, we go to the clarity of the New Testament, where the identity of the Messiah is revealed.

New Testament

The next passage to mention the name Messiah is found in the first chapter of John's gospel.

> One of the two who heard John speak, and followed Him, was Andrew, Simon Peter's brother. He found first his own brother Simon, and said to him, "We have found the *Messiah*" (which translated means Christ). (vv. 40–41, emphasis added)

And the last reference occurs in the dialogue between Jesus and the woman at the well, where He unmistakably claims the name for Himself.

> The woman said to Him, "Sir, I perceive that You are a prophet. Our fathers worshiped in this mountain, and you people say that in Jerusalem is the place where men ought to worship." Jesus said to her, "Woman, believe Me, an hour is coming when neither in this mountain, nor in Jerusalem, shall you worship the Father. You worship that which you do not know; we worship that which we know, for salvation is from the Jews. But an hour is coming, and now is, when the true worshipers shall worship the Father in spirit and truth; for such people the Father seeks to be His worshipers. God is spirit, and those who worship Him must worship in spirit and truth." The woman said to Him, "I know that *Messiah* is coming (He who is called Christ); when that One comes, He will declare all things to us." Jesus said to her, "I who speak to you am He." (4:19–26, emphasis added)

How the Name Emerged

Did you notice that each time you read the name Messiah in John, the phrases "means Christ" and "called Christ" were added?

That's because the Greek word for Christ, *christos*, is a translation of the Hebrew term *mashiach*, meaning Messiah. Simply put, Christ and Messiah are synonymous terms, and they share a common definition—"the Anointed One."[2]

To understand the historical background and significance of the title "the Anointed One," let's do a little etymological digging on *mashiach* and its Hebrew root, *mashach*.

Etymology

The verb *mashach* is found approximately 140 times in the Old Testament and is almost always rendered "to smear, anoint, spread." It was used to refer to something as plain as rubbing oil on a shield or to something as important as the religious ritual of applying "oil to items such as the tabernacle, altar or laver (Exod. 40:9–11), or even the sin offering (Exod. 29:36)."[3] More frequently, however, *mashach* was used

> for the ceremonial induction into leadership offices,
> an action which involved the pouring of oil from a
> horn upon the head of an individual.[4]

The three types of leaders who were anointed in this manner were prophets (1 Kings 19:16), priests (Exod. 28:40–41), and kings (1 Sam. 16:12–13).

Theology

We can uncover still more about the meaning of *mashach* by also examining its theological implications. First, an anointing proclaimed that someone was authorized to serve the Lord in a position of great honor and responsibility. Second, though the anointing ceremony may have been physically performed by a priest or a prophet, biblical writers often referred to God as the true anointing agent (see 1 Sam. 10:1). Such wording emphasized that the one being anointed was not to be harmed and was to be held in special regard (see 24:8–12; 26:6–12). Third, divine enablement accompanied *mashach*. "The Spirit of the Lord came mightily upon" both

---

2. Colin Brown, ed., *The New International Dictionary of New Testament Theology* (Grand Rapids, Mich.: Zondervan Publishing House, Regency Reference Library, 1975), vol. 1, p. 53.

3. R. Laird Harris, Gleason L. Archer, Jr., Bruce K. Waltke, eds., *Theological Wordbook of the Old Testament* (Chicago, Ill.: Moody Press, 1980), vol. 1, p. 530.

4. *Theological Wordbook of the Old Testament*, p. 530.

Saul and David in connection with their anointing (16:13; see also 10:6). And fourth, though many were anointed, only one would be *the* Anointed One, *mashiach*, through whom the destiny of the nation of Israel was to be fulfilled.[5]

The Emergence of the Messiah

All through Old Testament history, Israel anxiously awaited the arrival of the Messiah, the Anointed One whom they believed would immediately establish God's rule on earth forever.[6] That's why, when John the Baptizer came on the scene claiming "the kingdom of heaven is at hand" (Matt. 3:2), some thought that perhaps he was the Messiah.

> The people were in a state of expectation and all were wondering in their hearts about John, as to whether he might be the Christ. (Luke 3:15)

But John unhesitatingly set the people straight, pointing to the real Messiah instead (John 1:19–20, 29–36). And so it was that Andrew, one of John's disciples, followed Jesus and later excitedly told his brother Simon Peter, "We have found the Messiah" (v. 41). But did Peter believe him? Jesus Himself sought to know.

> Now when Jesus came into the district of Caesarea Philippi, He began asking His disciples, saying, "Who do people say that the Son of Man is?" And they said, "Some say John the Baptist; and others, Elijah; but still others, Jeremiah, or one of the prophets." He said to them, "But who do you say that I am?" And Simon Peter answered and said, "Thou art the Christ, the Son of the living God." (Matt. 16:13–16)

Thus far we've noted that the prophets predicted a Messiah, that John proclaimed His arrival, and that Andrew and Peter believed they had found Him. But what about Jesus? What was His

---

5. *Theological Wordbook of the Old Testament*, p. 530.

6. It's easy to see why the Jewish people fervently anticipated a Messiah when one considers the number of prophecies in the Old Testament that point to His coming. Alfred Edersheim, for example, lists 456 in his book *The Life and Times of Jesus the Messiah*. Even so, he still felt compelled to add the disclaimer, "Despite all labor and care, it can scarcely be hoped that the list is quite complete." Alfred Edersheim, *The Life and Times of Jesus the Messiah* (Grand Rapids, Mich.: William B. Eerdmans Publishing Co., n.d.), p. 710.

own testimony about Himself? On a visit back to His hometown synagogue, Jesus poignantly revealed the truth about His identity.

> And He came to Nazareth, where He had been brought up; and as was His custom, He entered the synagogue on the Sabbath, and stood up to read. And the book of the prophet Isaiah was handed to Him. And He opened the book, and found the place where it was written,
>
> "The Spirit of the Lord is upon Me,
> Because He anointed Me to preach the
>   Gospel to the poor.
> He has sent Me to proclaim release to the
>   captives,
> And recovery of sight to the blind,
> To set free those who are downtrodden,
> To proclaim the favorable year of the
>   Lord."
>
> And He closed the book, and gave it back to the attendant, and sat down; and the eyes of all in the synagogue were fixed upon Him. And He began to say to them, "Today this Scripture has been fulfilled in your hearing." (Luke 4:16–21; see also 24:25–27, 44–48)

The long-awaited Anointed One had come at last, bringing good news, release, and relief—precious gifts that only the Messiah, the Christ, could bring.

When We Acknowledge Jesus as Messiah

We often speak of Jesus Christ as if Christ were His second name. But as we have seen, it's really a title, a description. Jesus is *the* Christ, the Anointed One, and when we acknowledge Him as Messiah . . .

We claim Him to be the Anointed One. There is no other. He alone is the fulfillment of God's promised Redeemer.

We declare that our search for any and all other so-called Messiahs has ended. When Jesus asked His disciples if they wanted to leave Him, Peter answered, "Lord, to whom shall we go? You have words of eternal life" (John 6:68). For the disciples, the search was over; they had found the Messiah. And we affirm this same truth each time we call Him Christ.

22

We announce that He alone provides us with all we need for lasting satisfaction. No one can lift you from the deepest despair like Christ. As Corrie ten Boom's sister Betsie put it, "There is no pit so deep that He is not deeper still."[7] That's Messiah.

Our Father,

> *Bring to our minds afresh the significance of Your marvelous salvation for Your people. Humble us with the incredible truth that You sent the Christ, the Anointed One, to lay down His life so that we might have life in You. Thank You for the great love with which You love us, and may we return that love through grateful obedience this day. Amen.*

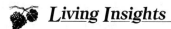 **Living Insights**   STUDY ONE

Let's see for ourselves how Jesus' birth, life, and death fulfilled the prophecies concerning the coming Messiah.

Read the verses in each section, and then draw a line from the prophecy to the passage that fulfills it.

Prophecy	_Fulfillment_
Birth	
Isaiah 7:14	Matthew 2:1
Micah 5:2	Matthew 2:1, 11
Psalm 72:10	Matthew 1:18, 24–25
Life	
Isaiah 11:2	Luke 19:35–37a
Isaiah 35:5–6a	Matthew 9:35
Zechariah 9:9	Matthew 3:16–17

---

7. Corrie ten Boom, with John and Elizabeth Sherrill, *The Hiding Place* (New York, N.Y.: Bantam Books; Old Tappan, N.J.: Fleming H. Revell Co., 1971), p. 217.

Death

Isaiah 53:7	John 19:34
Isaiah 53:5	Matthew 27:57–60
Psalm 22:18	Matthew 27:12
Isaiah 53:9	Matthew 27:35

These are but a few of the many inspired prophecies that were fulfilled by Jesus, proving that He is the Messiah. For as Josh McDowell points out in his book *Evidence That Demands a Verdict*:

> "The chance that any man might have lived down to the present time and fulfilled . . . eight prophecies is 1 in 10^{17}." That would be 1 in 100,000,000,000, 000,000. In order to help us comprehend this staggering probability, [Peter] Stoner illustrates it by supposing that "we take 10^{17} silver dollars and lay them on the face of Texas. They will cover all of the state two feet deep. Now mark one of these silver dollars and stir the whole mass thoroughly, all over the state. Blindfold a man and tell him that he can travel as far as he wishes, but he must pick up one silver dollar and say that this is the right one. What chance would he have of getting the right one? Just the same chance that the prophets would have had of writing . . . eight prophecies and having them all come true in any one man, from their day to the present time."[8]

🍇 *Living Insights*   STUDY TWO

To guide our worship of Jesus as Messiah, let's pause to let commentator William Barclay focus our attention on how Jesus fulfilled the anointed office of priest.

> The function of a priest is to open the way to God for men. The Latin word for *priest* is *pontifex*, which

---

8. Peter W. Stoner, *Science Speaks* (Chicago, Ill.: Moody Press, 1963), as quoted by Josh McDowell in *Evidence That Demands a Verdict*, rev. ed. (San Bernardino, Calif.: Here's Life Publishers, 1979), p. 167.

means a *bridge-builder.* The priest is the man who builds a bridge between men and God.

That is what Jesus did. He opened the way to God; he made it possible for men to enter into the very presence of God.[9]

Next read Romans 5:8–11; and then enter the very presence of God by the bridge that He has made possible, and give Him thanks and praise for what He has done.

Journal

_____

_____

_____

_____

_____

_____

_____

_____

_____

_____

_____

_____

9. William Barclay, *The Gospel of Matthew,* vol. 1, rev. ed., The Daily Study Bible Series (Philadelphia, Pa.: Westminster Press, 1975), p. 32.

Chapter 4

THE DAY GOD ANSWERED, "AMEN"

Selected Scriptures

Imagine for a moment that you are a Jew back in first-century Jerusalem. Life has been good to you—you have your own business, a large family, you attend synagogue—but still, something is missing. In your heart you have questions, doubts. Ever since that prophet, Jesus, was crucified, you've felt unsettled. You remember how he stirred your heart like no other when he spoke. Could he have been the Messiah after all? The chief priests and Pharisees condemned him, and that should have settled any doubts. But it hasn't. Finally, you invite the one follower of Jesus you know to share his story with you. So he has come to your shop, and this is his story.

———————◆———————

What happened that day is not easy to tell.

I remember that, for the first time since I was a child, I felt afraid of the dark. Something about the unnatural blackness that blotted out the midday sun was evil, ominous. When the Roman soldiers lit their torches, it was as though the light shone into the darkest pit of hell; and there I saw three men, gasping, bleeding, enveloped in an unholy cacophony of curses and insults.

The nightmarish horror of the crucifixions made me want to run and hide. And yet, at the same time, I felt strangely pulled toward the repulsive scene. For I had met the man in the middle . . . the one called Jesus.

It was years ago, when I first took over my family's business in Jerusalem. The shop needed some carpentry work, and a friend told me about a father-son business that did a good job for a reasonable price. A deal was struck, and that was when I first met Joseph and his son Jesus.

Many years passed before I was to see him again. During that time, I became a successful shopkeeper on one of Jerusalem's busiest streets. I loved haggling with people, whether it was over money or the latest gossip. You can imagine how surprised I was when I

This message was not part of the original series but is compatible with it.

began hearing about the same carpenter's son who had worked in my shop supposedly changing water into wine and walking on water! And then there was my close friend, Mattathias, who burst into my shop still shaking with the news that he had heard the voice of God saying that Jesus was His Son. "Such nonsense!" I said. "Who could believe it?"

To me, it was just the beginning of another wild rumor about the Messiah. Another impostor claiming to be the Anointed One. No doubt the Romans would kill or scare into silence this would-be Messiah too. So maybe you can understand my skepticism.

Over the next three years, the stories about Jesus continued to pour into my shop. There were fantastic tales of incredible miracles and tense confrontations with the religious rulers. The miracles I never saw; but I did see Pharisees, since several came by my shop regularly. And they were enraged by this "Galilean mountebank," as they called him. Which, by the way, wasn't any worse than some of the things I was told he called them. I sympathized with them because it was bad business to alienate the Pharisees. Still, I didn't really object to the things I heard about Jesus, even though I couldn't bring myself to take much of it seriously. Mostly I tried to stay out of the controversy and just concern myself with business . . . until that one strange, glorious day.

It was the time of the Passover, and my shop had been brimming all week with sojourners come to celebrate the holy day. But that afternoon, a change suddenly took place in the crowd outside my shop. People were lining both sides of the street, as if expecting to see a passing Roman potentate or a religious parade. Then they began to shout so loud that I couldn't hear myself talk inside the shop. Everyone hurried outside, including me, and this is what I heard ringing all up and down my street.

> "Hosanna!
> Blessed is He who comes in the name of the Lord;
> Blessed is the coming kingdom of our father David;
> Hosanna in the highest!"

I quickly threaded my way to the front of the crowd to see what was happening. The shouting became a roar of hysteria as a man riding a donkey approached. People everywhere were throwing branches from trees and cloaks from shoulders onto the road before this peculiar procession of one.

"Who is it?" I shouted to an excited stranger next to me.

27

"It's the prophet from Nazareth," he cried with tears in his eyes, "the Son of David!" And then he flung his expensive coat into the street just as the lone figure came near.

When I turned to look at the prophet's face, I found him staring at mine. It was Jesus. The boy had become a man, but still I recognized him. And I think he recognized me too, since he smiled at me with a gentle nod of acquaintance. Just then I felt an arm around my shoulder, and the giant fellow next to me nearly burst my eardrums as he bellowed,

> "Blessed is the King who comes in the name of the
>   Lord;
> Peace in heaven and glory in the highest!"

I didn't know what to think or say. All this time that I had been hearing about Jesus, he was just a story to tell, a theory to argue. Now he was real, right in front of me with hundreds, perhaps even thousands, heaping praises upon him. Children were dancing and cheering in a rain of praise that had completely washed all sadness and despair from the crowd . . . from me!

"Hosanna to the Son of David, blessed is the King of Israel!" I shouted at the top of my lungs. Me! And it felt wonderful. I couldn't stop shouting and smiling even as the crowd folded in behind Jesus and continued down the street. I just stood there shouting "hosanna!", lost in a joy I had never felt before. Finally, the solitary echo of my own voice snapped my reverie; and I noticed Ben Shamon, the shopkeeper across the street, standing there with arms akimbo, staring at me with a look of utter disbelief. Suddenly I felt very foolish and hurried inside.

For the next few days, Jesus took Jerusalem by storm. He threw the greedy money changers out of the temple and thwarted every attempt of the disgruntled Pharisees to discredit him. Nothing they did could sway the people from hanging on his every word. There were rumors that he was about to establish his rule as the Messiah. It seemed as if the whole city was intoxicated with anticipation, ready to be reborn at Jesus' signal into that golden era of Jehovah's righteous rule. And even though I had chided myself for getting caught up in that scene in the street, I still couldn't deny that I had become intrigued by this Galilean. My cynicism loosened just enough for me to secretly wonder, Could he really be the One?

Then it happened. I had just entered my shop early one morning, when Diosthenes appeared. He was the Greek who owned the tent shop next door. His visits were rare, and even more rarely did he have anything good to say.

"Greetings, Diosthenes," I said.

"Well, they got him."

"I'm fine, thank you. And you?"

"It was one of his own."

"Wait . . . what are you talking about?"

"You know, the Galilean, the one who's been parading around talking as if he were a god himself. They arrested him last night after one of his disciples turned him in."

"What? Are you sure it was Jesus?"

"Absolutely. They caught him hiding right there in Gethsemane. I heard that when they tried to arrest him he started a scuffle and cut off some poor fellow's ear. They finally had to tie him up."

"What have they done with him?"

"My cousin says he's been on trial all night long because the chief priests and Pharisees are in a hurry to get him crucified."

Crucified. The word struck me like a stone. Diosthenes left, and my thoughts reeled from the awful impact of his news. Was Jesus a hoax, just another pretender out to con everyone? At first my head pounded with a furious anger. I wanted to forget that he ever existed, that I had ever shouted "hosanna" or held the slightest hope that he might have been the Messiah. "He deserves to be crucified," I tried to convince myself. But the words were hollow. They weren't really what was in my heart. But why would Jesus allow all this to happen if he truly was the Messiah?

"Lord, what's happening?" I prayed. "Is he . . . no, it's impossible!" I could not believe or disbelieve. Hours later, the only thing I felt I could do, must do, was go see him at the place where criminals were crucified, Skull Hill.

As I arrived, the Roman soldiers were pounding the spikes into the hands and feet of not one, but three convicted men. Agonizing cries of tortured men mingled with the wails of inconsolable women. I felt unnerved and sickened by the sounds. When they lifted up the crosses, the crowd began brutally tearing at Jesus with their taunts, like jackals moving in for the kill. "He saved others, but he can't save himself! . . . Save yourself, come down from the cross, if you are the Son of God!"

I couldn't bring myself to draw too close. And even though I could tell which one was Jesus by the way they taunted him, physically I couldn't recognize him. They had beaten him too badly for that.

Then the midday darkness came. Night swallowed up the sun, sky, trees, hill, people, crosses; everything was erased into one vast oblivion. An eerie silence ensued in that nothingness, punctuated only by the painful gasps of the dying.

The soldiers quickly lit torches. The crowd seemed nervous, afraid. But then someone cursed the Nazarene, blaming him for this bad omen. A second voice agreed, and a third, and slowly you could sense the fear release itself in mockings that grew bolder and more hateful under the cover of darkness.

"Enough!" I thought. I wanted to leave, to run from this frightful obscenity. But, as in a boyhood nightmare, I couldn't move my legs. I stood transfixed by the horrible sight. Minutes passed, hours, and suddenly Jesus hurled a wail of chilling despair into the blackness.

"Eloi, Eloi, lama sabachthani?"

The man next to me thought he was calling for Elijah. "No," I whispered, "He calls God." And I remember shuddering as I translated Jesus' desperate words aloud, "My God, my God, why have You abandoned me?"

What does this mean? Was he the Messiah, but now God had abandoned him? Why? My mind whirled when the man beside me asked, "Did you hear about the suicide last night?"

"No."

"One of his disciples hung himself. He's been abandoned all right, by both God and that ignorant rabble he called his disciples. I heard that every one of them deserted him. I knew he wasn't no Messiah. Messiahs don't reign from bloody crosses, do they?" and he grinned.

I turned in disgust and immediately noticed a hyssop branch with a sponge on it being lifted up to Jesus. I moved closer to see what was happening. Again, Jesus spoke with a loud voice, "It is finished!" Incredibly, he said it as one would shout for joy at a victory just won. What victory? And then he said, in a final thunderous cry, "Father, into Your hands I commit my spirit," and it was over; he was dead, and I felt completely undone and confused.

I began to weep when, suddenly, I felt the earth shudder and begin to shake uncontrollably as if it, too, were in anguish over his death. People started running in every direction, fleeing, falling, yelling for help. Huge rocks split apart, hurling fragments into the terrified crowd. Everyone was afraid, including the awestruck Roman centurion who said, "Truly, this was the Son of God!"

Son of God? Messiah? For the next two days and into the early morning hours of the Sabbath, I could hardly sleep, haunted by that horrible event. Was Jesus the Messiah? Why did God forsake him? What did he finish? "Great Adonai," I pled, "who was that man in the middle?"

Then I remembered something my friend Mattathias had said the day he rushed into my shop with the news about God naming Jesus as His Son. He had also related how the prophet John the Baptist had pointed at Jesus and said, "Behold, the Lamb of God who takes away the sin of the world!"

Lamb . . . *lamb*. I had seen thousands offered on the temple altar as the sacrificial atonement for our sins. Blood was shed and— wait, that's it! That's it! That's what Jesus' crucifixion was all about. Why hadn't I understood this before? Jesus was God's human lamb, a sinless sacrifice. It's just as the rabbi had read from the prophet Isaiah last Saturday:

> He was oppressed and He was afflicted,
> Yet He did not open His mouth;
> Like a lamb that is led to slaughter,
> And like a sheep that is silent before its shearers,
> So He did not open His mouth. . . .
> Surely our griefs He Himself bore,
> And our sorrows He carried;
> Yet we ourselves esteemed Him stricken,
> Smitten of God, and afflicted.
> But He was pierced through for our transgressions,
> He was crushed for our iniquities;
> The chastening for our well-being fell upon Him,
> And by His scourging we are healed.
> All of us like sheep have gone astray,
> Each of us has turned to his own way;
> But the Lord has caused the iniquity of us all
> To fall on Him.

No sooner had I begun to grasp these truths than the house began to shake in a second violent earthquake. It was only later that I learned it was caused by the angel who descended that morning and rolled away the stone from Jesus' grave. To me it was like God saying, "Amen" to His Son's victory cry, "It is finished!" Jesus *was* the Messiah. And He is risen!

Before you go back to your own shopkeeping chores and life-as-usual routines, consider an important question posed by Max Lucado in his poignant book *No Wonder They Call Him the Savior.*

> The immensity of the Nazarene's execution makes it impossible to ignore. . . . Everybody has an opinion. Everyone is choosing a side. You can't be neutral on an issue like this one. Apathy? Not this time. It's one side or the other. All have to choose.
>
> And choose they did.
>
> For every cunning Caiaphas there was a daring Nicodemus. For every cynical Herod there was a questioning Pilate. For every pot-mouthed thief there was a truth-seeking one. For every turncoat Judas there was a faithful John.
>
> There was something about the crucifixion that made every witness either step toward it or away from it. It simultaneously compelled and repelled.
>
> And today, two thousand years later, the same is true. It's the watershed. It's the Continental Divide. It's Normandy. And you are either on one side or the other. A choice is demanded. We can do what we want with the cross. We can examine its history. We can study its theology. We can reflect upon its prophecies. Yet the one thing we can't do is walk away in neutral. No fence sitting is permitted. The cross, in its absurd splendor, doesn't allow that. That is one luxury that God, in his awful mercy, doesn't permit.
>
> On which side are you?[1]

🍇 Living Insights

"On which side are you?" Chances are, if you chose this guide to study, you already know Jesus as the Messiah. You're on the believing side, the side that has eternal life.

---

1. Max Lucado, *No Wonder They Call Him the Savior* (Portland, Oreg.: Multnomah Press, 1986), pp. 72–73.

But what about those others who are still in the dark? What will become of that family member? That neighbor? On which side is your boss? Your friend? Who's going to love them sacrificially and wage war for them spiritually through prayer so that they might see and know that Jesus is the Messiah?

Pause for a moment to reflect on your family members, neighbors, coworkers, and friends to see if there is someone you could commit yourself to loving and praying for faithfully. If a specific name comes to mind, write it down in the space provided.

Jesus sacrificed Himself so that this person might live. What will you sacrifice?

🍇 *Living Insights*

To help you focus your heart on Jesus so that you can worship Him as the Messiah, here's a powerful excerpt from Max Lucado's book *No Wonder They Call Him the Savior,* called "Take Me Home."

> *"Father, into your hands I commit my spirit"*
> Luke 23:46.

Were it a war—this would be the aftermath.
Were it a symphony—this would be the second
                                    between the final note and
                                    the first applause.
Were it a journey—this would be the sight of
                                    home.
Were it a storm—this would be the sun, piercing
                                    the clouds.
But it wasn't. It was a Messiah. And this was a
        sigh of joy.

"Father!" (The voice is hoarse.)
The voice that called forth the dead,
the voice that taught the willing,
the voice that screamed at God,
        now says, "Father!"
        "Father."

The two are again one.

The abandoned is now found.
The schism is now bridged.

"Father." He smiles weakly. "It's over."
Satan's vultures have been scattered.
Hell's demons have been jailed.
Death has been damned.
The sun is out,
The Son is out.

It's over.
An angel sighs. A star wipes away a tear.

"Take me home."
Yes, take him home.
Take this prince to his king
Take this son to his father
Take this pilgrim to his home
(He deserves a rest.)

"Take me home."
Come ten thousand angels! Come and take this
wounded troubador to
the cradle of his Father's arms!

Farewell manger's infant
Bless You holy ambassador
Go Home death slayer
Rest well sweet soldier

The battle is over.[2]

| Journal |

_____

_____

_____

_____

_____

_____

2. Lucado, *No Wonder They Call Him the Savior,* pp. 65–66.

Chapter 5

HE'S THE ALPHA
AND THE OMEGA

Revelation 1:18; 21:6; 22:13

In *The Glorious Names of Jesus,* Amos R. Wells writes:

> We think so often of the Savior as the Man of
> Galilee that it is hard to think of him as the Ancient
> of Days, the Creator, with the Father in the begin-
> ning, he without whom nothing was made that was
> made. We have gazed so long upon the Redeemer as
> he hung upon the cross outside the wall of Jerusalem
> that we find it difficult to realize that he is also the
> Lamb slain from the foundation of the world. We
> localize him in place and time, and that is well; that
> is why he was incarnated, that we might do that very
> thing, that he might become Immanuel, God with
> us. But in the process we are likely to narrow our
> thought of him, and sadly to miss his infinite scope.[1]

It is our hope that this study will enable your thoughts to go
beyond the narrow scope of human understanding and soar into the
infinite character revealed in the name *the Alpha and the Omega.*

References in Scripture: A Brief Observation

Throughout all sixty-six books of the Bible, the title the Alpha
and the Omega appears only three times. And all three references
are found in the same book, Revelation. Before we examine those
passages, however, let's turn to the book of Isaiah to get a glimpse
of the fullness of this name's meaning.

Old Testament

Though the title the Alpha and the Omega is not mentioned
in Isaiah, the meaning behind the name is revealed through the
words of the Lord Jehovah Himself.

1. Amos R. Wells, *The Glorious Names of Jesus* (New York, N.Y.: Fleming H. Revell Co.,
1926), p. 45.

35

"Coastlands, listen to Me in silence,
And let the peoples gain new strength;
Let them come forward, then let them speak;
Let us come together for judgment.
Who has aroused one from the east
Whom He calls in righteousness to His feet?
He delivers up nations before him,
And subdues kings.
He makes them like dust with his sword,
As the wind-driven chaff with his bow.
He pursues them, passing on in safety,
By a way he had not been traversing with his feet.
Who has performed and accomplished it,
Calling forth the generations from the beginning?
'I, the Lord, am the first, and with the last.
    I am He.'"
(41:1–4)

Another layer of meaning becomes visible in the Lord's description of Himself in chapter 44.

"Thus says the Lord, the King of Israel
And his Redeemer, the Lord of hosts:
'I am the first and I am the last,
And there is no God besides Me.
And who is like Me? Let him proclaim and
    declare it;
Yes, let him recount it to Me in order,
From the time that I established the ancient
    nation.
And let them declare to them the things that are
    coming
And the events that are going to take place.'"
(vv. 6–7)

And, finally, in chapter 48, we are given another glimpse into the substance of this glorious name.

"Listen to Me, O Jacob, even Israel whom I called;
I am He, I am the first, I am also the last.
Surely My hand founded the earth,
And My right hand spread out the heavens;
When I call to them, they stand together."
(vv. 12–13)

Crossing over to the New Testament book of Revelation, we'll find Alpha and Omega in three passages, the first being 1:8. Here the title is clearly attributed to God the Father.

> "I am the Alpha and the Omega," says the Lord God, "who is and who was and who is to come, the Almighty." (v. 8)

Notice how God amplifies His name in the words "who is"—that's the present; "who was"—the past; and "who is to come"—the future. These descriptions reveal God's all-encompassing nature, showing that in His being lies the totality of all existence.

This same name is used of the Father again later, in the epochal scene depicted by the apostle John in the first seven verses of chapter 21.

> And I saw a new heaven and a new earth; for the first heaven and the first earth passed away, and there is no longer any sea. And I saw the holy city, new Jerusalem, coming down out of heaven from God, made ready as a bride adorned for her husband. And I heard a loud voice from the throne, saying, "Behold, the tabernacle of God is among men, and He shall dwell among them, and they shall be His people, and God Himself shall be among them, and He shall wipe away every tear from their eyes; and there shall no longer be any death; there shall no longer be any mourning, or crying, or pain; the first things have passed away." And He who sits on the throne said, "Behold, I am making all things new." And He said, "Write, for these words are faithful and true." And He said to me, "It is done. I am the Alpha and the Omega, the beginning and the end. I will give to the one who thirsts from the spring of the water of life without cost. He who overcomes shall inherit these things, and I will be his God and he will be My son."

There is one last reference to Alpha and Omega, and it is unique in that this "title which is the title of God is given unhesitatingly and without qualification to Jesus Christ."[2]

2. William Barclay, *Jesus as They Saw Him* (1962; reprint, Grand Rapids, Mich.: William B. Eerdmans Publishing Co., 1980), p. 380.

"Behold, I am coming quickly, and My reward is with Me, to render to every man according to what he has done. I am the Alpha and the Omega, the first and the last, the beginning and the end." Blessed are those who wash their robes, that they may have the right to the tree of life, and may enter by the gates into the city. . . .

"I, Jesus, have sent My angel to testify to you these things for the churches. I am the root and the offspring of David, the bright morning star." (22:12–14, 16)

Examination of the Meaning

Now that we've met this name for Christ through these passages of Scripture, our next step is to thoroughly examine its meaning. To begin, let's see how the concept developed in the Hebrew world of the Old Testament.

Hebrew Concept

Using the first and last letters of the Hebrew alphabet, *aleph* and *tau*, rabbis used to say that

> Adam transgressed the law from *aleph* to *tau* and Abraham kept the law from *aleph* to *tau*. The rabbis said that when God blessed his people, he blessed them from *aleph* to *tau*.[3]

"From *aleph* to *tau*"—from beginning to end and everything in between. This Hebrew phrase communicates the idea of completion, as well as the concept of continuation. One example of this idea is seen in the story of Joshua assuming the leadership of Israel after Moses' death. It was an extremely critical time; the young nation was about to enter the Promised Land—and many wars. You can imagine the anxiety the people must have felt at losing the one who had miraculously led them for the past forty years. Joshua certainly felt the loss, perhaps even more so since God had chosen him to fill Moses' sandals. In Joshua 1, however, God reassured Joshua that He would continue and complete all His promises to Israel under Joshua's leadership, just as He had under Moses'.

---

3. Barclay, *Jesus as They Saw Him*, p. 381.

"Moses My servant is dead; now therefore arise, cross this Jordan, you and all this people, to the land which I am giving to them, to the sons of Israel. Every place on which the sole of your foot treads, I have given it to you, just as I spoke to Moses. From the wilderness and this Lebanon, even as far as the great river, the river Euphrates, all the land of the Hittites, and as far as the Great Sea toward the setting of the sun, will be your territory. No man will be able to stand before you all the days of your life. *Just as I have been with Moses, I will be with you; I will not fail you or forsake you.*" (vv. 2–5, emphasis added)

A. W. Tozer heightens the significance of this passage for us.

We cannot think rightly of God until we begin to think of Him as always being *there*, and *there first*. Joshua had this to learn. He had been so long the servant of God's servant Moses, and had with such assurance received God's word at his mouth, that Moses and the God of Moses had become blended in his thinking, so blended that he could hardly separate the two thoughts; by association they always appeared together in his mind. Now Moses is dead, and lest the young Joshua be struck down with despair God spoke to assure him, "As I was with Moses, so I will be with thee." Moses was dead, but the God of Moses still lived. Nothing had changed and nothing had been lost. Nothing of God dies when a man of God dies. . . .

Here we acknowledge (and there is fear and wonder in the thought) the essential unity of God's nature, the timeless persistence of His changeless Being throughout eternity and time. Here we begin to see and feel the Eternal Continuum. Begin where we will, God is there first. He is Alpha and Omega.[4]

Greek Concept

This same concept of continuous involvement and power translates in Greek as *alpha* and *omega*, the first and last letter of the

---

4. A. W. Tozer, *The Divine Conquest* (Camp Hill, Pa.: Christian Publications, 1978), pp. 20–21.

Greek alphabet. Both *aleph* to *tau* and *alpha* to *omega* describe perfect continuity, something that has no break, is unchanging and uninterrupted.[5]

One final point to consider comes from Revelation 22:13, where Jesus states that He is "the beginning and the end." The Greek words for *beginning* and *end* respectively are *archē* and *telos*. *Archē* can mean "beginning in point of time" and also "beginning in the sense of origin." *Telos*, on the other hand, can mean "ending in a point of time" and also "ending in the sense of goal or consummation." Together these two words signify that Jesus is the source, the origin, the One from whom life originated; and He's the ultimate end, the final goal toward which all of life is moving.[6]

Practical Significance

What is the practical side of understanding this title? Knowing Jesus as the Alpha and the Omega keeps us from feeling like we're the product of chance, that we're left to fight for survival and then pass into oblivion. His name assures us that there is purpose and meaning behind all of life. Nothing occurs that is outside His awareness or involvement.

Realms in Which the "Alpha-Omega" Is Involved

The active, omnipotent presence of the Alpha and Omega becomes strikingly visible in four particular realms.

First: *The very presence of life.* Neither our birth nor our death is an accident. The Alpha and Omega knows fully the end from the beginning for each one of us. Our very breath is under His sovereign supervision (Job 12:9–10).

Second: *The ultimate purpose of our existence.* He knows why we are placed here, what we are to do, and where it finally all leads (see Acts 17:26–27).

Third: *The circumstances of our surroundings.* The name Alpha and Omega suggests that He is involved in the full spectrum of events, from the good to the bad, the prosperous to the calamitous, the gain to the loss, the expected to the unexpected (see Rom. 11:36).

And fourth: *The results of our efforts.* What may be unappreciated or insignificant in the world's eyes will not escape the notice of the

5. See Barclay, *Jesus as They Saw Him,* p. 382.

6. See Barclay, *Jesus as They Saw Him,* pp. 382–83.

Alpha and Omega, the "author and perfecter" of our faith (see Heb. 12:1– 2a). He will reward each of us on the final Judgment Day according to our works; so, as Paul admonishes, "Be steadfast, immovable, always abounding in the work of the Lord, knowing that your toil is not in vain in the Lord" (1 Cor. 15:58).

Conclusion

From an earthly point of view, Jesus' crucifixion seems a complete contradiction of all that we have learned about the name the Alpha and the Omega. And yet, at the moment when He appeared least in control of the presence of His own life, the purpose of His own existence, the circumstances of His own surroundings, and the results of His own efforts, He was actually fulfilling God's perfect pattern for our salvation. Even then He was in complete control from start to finish, beginning to end, from *alpha* to *omega*.

Our Father,

> For the very presence of our lives, the ultimate purpose of our existence, your presence in the circumstances that surround us, and the results of our efforts, we pause to express our gratitude. Thank You for caring enough to stoop and meet us in our need, for sending Jesus to cleanse us from our sins with His blood. We come to worship, to celebrate, to reflect, to acknowledge You as the Alpha and the Omega, the beginning and the end. In Jesus' wonderful name. Amen.

Living Insights   STUDY ONE

One personal, warm fact of Jesus' character as revealed in His name the Alpha and the Omega is that He is always present with us. Yet many of us are not comforted by this reality because we have failed to grasp the truth of it. As A. W. Tozer incisively observed:

> We talk of Him much and loudly, but we secretly think of Him as being absent, and we think of ourselves as inhabiting a parenthetic interval between the God who was and the God who will be. And

we are lonely with an ancient and cosmic loneliness. We are each like a little child lost in a crowded market, who has strayed but a few feet from its mother, yet because she cannot be seen the child is inconsolable. So we try by every method devised . . . to relieve our fears and heal our hidden sadness; but with all our efforts we remain unhappy still, with the settled despair of men alone in a vast and deserted universe.[7]

When all the activity ceases, when no one is around and there's no place to go, do you feel like a little child lost in a crowded market? Do you feel a gnawing sense of loneliness? If so, write down the methods you have devised to relieve that loneliness.

Many of us rely on relationships, television, movies, constant activities, even food to repress the loneliness we feel. But these were never designed to heal our loneliness. What is the cure? Again, let's listen to Tozer.

In my creature impatience I am often caused to wish that there were some way to bring modern Christians into a deeper spiritual life painlessly by short easy lessons; but such wishes are vain. No short cut exists. God has not bowed to our nervous haste nor embraced the methods of our machine age. It is well that we accept the hard truth now: *the man who would know God must give time to Him.* He must count no time wasted which is spent in the cultivation of His acquaintance.[8]

Possessing the comfort of His presence instead of a desperate sense of loneliness is possible if we are willing to give time to Him. Are you willing? If so, give Him your time and attention right

7. Tozer, *The Divine Conquest*, p. 23.

8. Tozer, *The Divine Conquest*, p. 22.

now—begin to wean yourself from those devices with which you've tried to relieve your loneliness and replace them with things that will bring you closer to Him. These could be times spent in quiet and reflective Bible reading, prayer that listens as well as speaks, restorative walks in nature's revelation, reverent and focused church attendance—even a searching season through counseling's paths of truth. Remember, "no time [is] wasted which is spent in the cultivation of His acquaintance."

🍇 Living Insights STUDY TWO

Alpha . . . let's enter into worship of this aspect of Jesus' nature by reading a meditation from Mary Loeks' book *The Glorious Names of God.*

> Time had a beginning. Creation had a beginning. We had a beginning. Civilizations have a beginning. Books have a beginning. All of the endeavors we would undertake have their beginning.
>
> But God? God has no beginning. Before any other beginning began, he was. "Before Abraham was born, I am!" declared Jesus (John 8:58). Why, then, would the eternal God have named himself Alpha, the first letter of the Greek alphabet, the beginning? It must have been because he is the great Beginner of all other beginnings! "Through him all things were made; without him nothing was made that has been made" (John 1:3).
>
> Alpha, God: We lay before you that which we will attempt to begin this day. We acknowledge that without you, all our attempts at beginnings are in vain. We can't see what will result from that which we now begin. Apprehension is mixed with our enthusiasm. We place it before you, Alpha, God, knowing that you see not just the beginning, but the whole.
>
> We worship you, we build our lives upon you, our Alpha God, who is truly without beginning.[9]

9. Mary Foxwell Loeks, *The Glorious Names of God* (Grand Rapids, Mich.: Baker Book House, 1986), pp. 13–14.

Continue now with your own meditation and prayer. Give Him time and He will draw near, for He is a "rewarder of those who seek Him" (Heb. 11:6; see also James 4:8a).

$$\boxed{\textbf{Journal}}$$

_____

_____

_____

_____

_____

_____

_____

_____

_____

_____

_____

_____

_____

_____

_____

_____

_____

Chapter 6

FOUR TITLES – SAME SAVIOR

Survey of the Four Gospels

The central theme of the Bible is indeed Jesus Christ. As one saint put it, "Cut the Scriptures anywhere and they bleed with the Lamb of God who takes away the sin of the world." He is the focal point. And the books of the Bible that focus completely on the Savior's life are commonly known as the Gospels.

The word *gospel* is derived from two words: *good* and *story*. Literally, it means "the good news" and is used to signify the wonderful message of forgiveness, reconciliation, and new life through Jesus Christ.

The four New Testament reporters who wrote the story of this good news are Matthew, a converted tax collector; Mark, a missionary; Luke, a physician; and John, a fisherman.

None of them, however, singly or together, give us a complete picture of Jesus (see John 21:25). Rather, each man provides us with snapshots of the Savior's life as seen through the lens of his own unique perspective. And even if you were to put all four together, you would still have something more like a slide presentation of Jesus' life than a comprehensive movie.

So, if we don't get a complete picture from their four accounts, then why do we have four Gospels? Let's take a moment to answer this question before going on to examine the picture each writer provides.

Why Four Gospels . . . Why Not Just One?

The simplest reason for having four Gospels is that one would not have been sufficient—it takes all four to give us a more balanced portrait of Christ. And we have great assurance that the portrait is indeed an accurate one because these men didn't write their stories on their own, but they wrote them through the divine inspiration of the Holy Spirit.[1]

---

1. God the Holy Spirit supernaturally assisted Matthew, Mark, Luke, and John, not only in compiling their facts, but also in the process of recording them (see 1 Cor. 2:6–13; 2 Tim. 3:16–17; 2 Pet. 1:20–21).

It's also important to note that each writer took great care in presenting the truth about his Savior, which is evident from the introduction of Luke's gospel.

> Inasmuch as many have undertaken to compile an account of the things accomplished among us, just as those who from the beginning were eyewitnesses and servants of the word have handed them down to us, it seemed fitting for me as well, having investigated everything carefully from the beginning, to write it out for you in consecutive order, most excellent Theophilus; so that you might know the exact truth about the things you have been taught. (Luke 1:1– 4)

Now let's step back and examine our wonderful Savior through the different and distinct angles of the four gospel writers.

How Did the Four Present Our Lord?

As we work our way through this brief survey, it will be helpful to remember that each author wrote with a different audience in mind. Matthew, for example, wrote primarily to Jews. Mark had Roman believers in mind, Luke was thinking of the Greeks, and John kept his an appeal to all people.

Matthew Saw Him as the Mighty King

More than any of the other gospel writers, Matthew seeks to convince his Jewish readers that Jesus is the Messiah, the promised king of Israel. He uses phrases like "so that what was spoken through the prophet might be fulfilled" at least nine times, showing that Jesus is the fulfillment of Old Testament prophecies. And he traces Christ's genealogy through the Jews' greatest king, David, and then back to the father of the Jewish nation, Abraham (Matt. 1:1–16). In fact, he emphasizes Jesus' royal lineage by using the name "Son of David" seven times in his book.

The theme of Christ's kingship is also seen in the thirty-two references to "the kingdom of heaven." And only Matthew records with such detail the kingdom lifestyle Jesus described in the Sermon on the Mount (Matt. 5–7).

Picking up on Matthew's theme of Jesus as the mighty King, commentator William Barclay notes:

Before Pilate, Jesus deliberately accepts the name of King (27:11). Even on the Cross the title of King is affixed, even if it be in mockery, over his head (27:37). . . . The final claim of Jesus is: "All authority has been given to me" (28:18).

Matthew's picture of Jesus is of the man born to be King. Jesus walks through his pages as if in the purple and gold of royalty.[2]

Mark Viewed Him as the Suffering Servant

Mark's picture of the Savior shows a different aspect of Jesus than Matthew's gospel—he sees him as actively engaged in serving His fellow man. Emphasizing Jesus' work, this gospel is largely a book of action. Reflecting this emphasis is Mark's constant use of the word *immediately*, highlighting many brief, action-packed accounts. For example, here is just a sampling of its use in the opening chapter.

> And immediately the Spirit impelled Him to go out into the wilderness. (Mark 1:12)

> And they immediately left the nets and followed Him. (v. 18)

> And immediately He called them; and they left their father Zebedee in the boat with the hired servants, and went away to follow Him. (v. 20)

> And immediately the news about Him went out everywhere into all the surrounding district of Galilee. (v. 28)

> And immediately after they had come out of the synagogue, they came into the house of Simon and Andrew, with James and John. (v. 29)

> And immediately the leprosy left him and he was cleansed. (v. 42)

Also, where Matthew starts his gospel by tracing Jesus' genealogy, Mark jumps right into the action—the start of Jesus' public ministry with His baptism by John.

2. William Barclay, *The Gospel of Matthew*, vol. 1, rev. ed., The Daily Study Bible Series (Philadelphia, Pa.: Westminster Press, 1975), p. 9.

The one statement that best summarizes Mark's active portrayal of Christ as a servant is found in 10:45:

> "For even the Son of Man did not come to be served,
> but to serve, and to give His life a ransom for many."

Doctor Luke Wrote of Him as the Ideal Man

As you might expect from a physician, Luke emphasizes the humanity of Christ in his gospel. When he lists Jesus' ancestry, for example, he takes us all the way back to Adam, linking Christ with all men. He also gives more details about Jesus' birth than any of the other gospel writers, and only he tells of Jesus' childhood.

In contrast to Mark's action-packed gospel, Luke continually brings before us human interest stories and the parables that Jesus shared. And when the Savior's death approaches, the doctor lingers much longer over the trials, the dialogue, and the whole process of the crucifixion than Mark does. Here you feel the blows of the beatings and the torture of the cross more than anywhere else.

Another unique aspect of Luke's gospel is his record of the Emmaus road experience. Only Luke writes of this post-resurrection appearance of Jesus as He revealed Himself in the Scriptures for the two disciples on that dusty road (24:13–35). And it's Luke who tells us how the ideal Man appeared to His disciples and calmed their fears concerning His resurrection with the words, "See My hands and My feet, that it is I Myself; touch Me and see, for a spirit does not have flesh and bones as you see that I have" (24:39).

John Presented Him as the Divine Son of God

The last gospel we come to was written well after the others, near the end of the first century. It was penned by John, the disciple whom Jesus loved. And it is near the end of his book that he reveals his purpose in writing.

> Many other signs therefore Jesus also performed in
> the presence of the disciples, which are not written
> in this book; but these have been written that you
> may believe that Jesus is the Christ, the Son of God;
> and that believing you may have life in His name.
> (20:30–31)

Jesus wasn't only a king, or merely a servant, or simply a man; He was the Lord God—deity—and He never stopped being God, even while on this earth. As evidence of this, John presents one miracle after another that only the divine Son of God could perform. Jesus turned water into wine (chap. 2). He healed the sick and the disabled (chaps. 4, 5, 9). He raised Lazarus from the dead (chap. 11).

In addition, only in John do you find Jesus' seven "I am's," revelations that, again, befit only God. For example, after feeding the five thousand, Jesus said, "I am the bread of life" (6:35, 41, 48, 51). Just before He raised Lazarus from the dead, Jesus told Martha, "I am the resurrection and the life" (11:25). In chapter 14, when the disciple Thomas said no one knew the way to the Father's house, Jesus responded with, "I am the way and the truth and the life" (v. 6).[3]

From the opening prologue,

> In the beginning was the Word, and the Word was with God, and the Word was God. . . .
> And the Word became flesh, and dwelt among us, and we beheld His glory, glory as of the only begotten from the Father, full of grace and truth. (1:1, 14)

to Thomas' confession in chapter 20, "My Lord and my God!" (v. 28), John's record creates the clear picture of Jesus as the divine Son of God.

In What Way Does This Apply to Us Today?

As you think about the four portraits of the same Savior the gospel writers have given us, remember that you also are posing for portraits—portraits of the different roles you fill in life. Perhaps you're a woman whose daily roles include being a wife, a mother, a daughter, an employee, and a Bible study leader. You may be a man, which may include being a son, a husband, or a father who must assume three different parenting roles for three children whose ages and needs vary. Whatever the roles you are facing right now, God desires that you live out each one for His glory.

Also, remember that God wants you to use each one of your roles to lead others to Christ. In your different realms of responsibility, do people see and hear enough to believe? Can others feel

---

3. The others are "I am the light of the world" (8:12; 9:5); "I am the door" (10:7, 9); "I am the good shepherd" (vv. 11, 14); "I am the true vine" (15:1, 5).

His gentle, healing touch in your role as a spouse or a parent? Can they hear His calm, compassionate voice— and His laughter—in your role as a grandparent, employee, single adult, or leader? Let your goal in each of the roles God has given you be like John's: that in seeing you, others may believe that Jesus is the Christ, the Son of God.

Our Father,

I confess, I believe, Jesus truly is the mighty King. He has set me free from sin's captivity, and I gratefully acknowledge His right to rule over me.

I am humbled that the King of Kings would come to serve and not to be served. Create in me such a heart; teach me to serve; show me whose feet I might wash today. Let me taste the sweet reward of fellowship with You as a lowly servant.

Let me touch You, Jesus; bid me also to come and see with the eyes of faith Your hands and feet. Oh, that I might be able to grasp the reality of Your presence and know the comfort of Your nearness.

Take away my blindness, Jesus, Son of God. Let me see clearly Your heavenly nature and glorious deity. Purge me of my doubts with a purifying conviction of Your divinity so that I, too, can exclaim, "My Lord and my God!" For Your name's sake, Amen.

🍇 Living Insights

Let's take a moment to reflect a little more deeply on the final two thoughts from our lesson. First, using the column on the left, write down the significant roles that you normally fill each week. For example, husband, wife, executive, parent, Sunday school teacher, and so forth.

Roles	1	2

Now, looking back at the roles you've just listed, examine your attitude and actions in each one with these two questions:

> 1. Am I fulfilling this role wholeheartedly, as if I were doing it just for God (see Col. 3:23–24)? Use the column marked *1* to record your answer.

> 2. Am I living as an ambassador for Christ in this role so that God might draw others to Jesus through me (see 2 Cor. 5:20)? Mark your answer in column 2.

From what you've indicated, is there one particular role in which you feel you're not glorifying God or being an authentic witness? If so, use the space provided to begin brainstorming a corrective measure you could put into action in the next several days.

Role:_____

Corrective measure: _____

_____

_____

_____

_____

_____

Often, when we think of the word *worship*, we associate it with giving praise, adoration, and thanksgiving through prayer and song. These are good and right, but there is an additional way of worshiping, one that the apostle Paul mentions in his letter to the Romans.

> I urge you therefore, brethren, by the mercies of God, to present your bodies a living and holy sacrifice, acceptable to God, which is your spiritual service of worship. (12:1)

True worship can also be expressed by our actions. We don't always need padded pews and pipe organs to offer praise to Jesus. As Paul reminds us, our whole lives, everything we do and say, either glorifies Him or doesn't (see also 1 Cor. 3:16).

With this in mind, we'd like to challenge you to think of some specific ways you can present your body as a living and holy sacrifice to worship Jesus as the mighty King, the suffering Servant, the ideal Man, and the Son of God. In what way could you obey Jesus as your King? What service could you perform today as an act of worship to the suffering Servant? Use the space provided to write down one specific act of worship you will commit to do this week.

Jesus, the mighty King _____

_____

Jesus, the suffering Servant_____

_____

Jesus, the ideal Man _____

_____

Jesus, the divine Son of God _____

_____

Evelyn Underhill defines worship as "the total adoring response of man to the one Eternal God."[4] Go, and let these promised acts of spiritual worship become an adoring response to your wonderful Savior.

___

4. As quoted by Warren W. Wiersbe, *Real Worship* (Nashville, Tenn.: Thomas Nelson Publishers, Oliver-Nelson Books, 1986), p. 21.

Journal

_____

_____

_____

_____

_____

_____

_____

_____

_____

_____

_____

_____

_____

_____

_____

_____

_____

_____

_____

Chapter 7

"I AM THE TRUE VINE"

John 15:1–11

Blink and you'll miss it. No, not a town, a name: "True Vine." In the 31,173 verses of the Bible,[1] this title appears in only one verse, one time. The writer who captured this momentary yet indelible image was the disciple whom Jesus loved, John.

Let's journey into the fifteenth chapter of his gospel, where we'll discover the meaning of this rare and unique title and what it teaches about our relationship with Christ our Lord.

General Observations of the Passage

Before we step inside our passage, let's take a broad look at its context. *First*, these verses were written for those who know Christ and need to abide in Him. The unsaved will find nothing here explaining the way of salvation.

Second, the truth of these verses clusters around the symbol of a vine and a branch, which Jesus uses metaphorically to describe our spiritual life in Him.

Third, the main subject is *abiding*. The theme of the passage is the branches' relationship to the vine.

And *fourth*, the result of abiding is bearing fruit. Jesus doesn't discuss salvation, which, in this metaphor, would be the root. Rather, He focuses on fruit, the kind that ripens in those who abide in Him. He describes four kinds of vines: those that do not bear fruit (v. 2a), those that bear fruit (v. 2b), those that bear more fruit (v. 2c), and those that bear much fruit (vv. 5, 8).

Specific Interpretations of Key Terms

Now that we have the general picture, let's examine the key terms that lay ahead in John 15:1–11, then develop the passage verse by verse.

---

1. H. L. Willmington, *Willmington's Book of Bible Lists* (Wheaton, Ill.: Tyndale House Publishers, 1987), pp. 34, 35.

Vine. In verse 1, Jesus clearly identifies Himself as the vine. In fact, He calls Himself the "true vine." The sentence structure in Greek emphasizes the adjective "true," making it read, "I am the vine, the true one!" He is the genuine and only source of life. All other vines are imitations.

Vinedresser. Also in verse 1, Jesus identifies the Father as the vinedresser. He is the gardener who works with the branches, doing all the cultivating, spading, and pruning (v. 2).

Branch. Even though branches are mentioned in verses 2–4, it's not until verse 5 that Jesus identifies them as believers.

Abide. Through verses 1–3, the focus is on production and pruning. In verses 4–11, however, we learn that the secret to fruit bearing is abiding. No abiding, no fruit.

Using all this information as a guide, let's return to verse 1 and slowly work our way through the passage.

> "I am the true vine, and My Father is the vine-dresser. Every branch in Me that does not bear fruit, He takes away; and every branch that bears fruit, He prunes it, that it may bear more fruit." (vv. 1–2)[2]

From these two verses emerges this one central truth: the vine is the source of life for the branch. A branch may bear the fruit, but it is the vine that actually produces it. What kind of fruit will the True Vine cause us to bear? The apostle Paul has the answer in Galatians 5.

> The fruit of the Spirit is love, joy, peace, patience, kindness, goodness, faithfulness, gentleness, self-control. (vv. 22–23a)

Working together with the Vine to ensure our fruitfulness is the Vinedresser, the Father. According to John 15:2, He accomplishes this through two different methods. First, He "takes away" those branches that aren't bearing any fruit. In Greek, the word for "takes away" means "to raise, take up, lift." People who work with vines say that a vine will not produce if it has fallen down into the dirt.

---

2. Jesus makes a distinction between those who are in Him (v. 2), and those who abide in Him (vv. 4–6). When we believed in Jesus for salvation, He grafted us into Himself and we became branches. Positionally, we are now "in Christ." But position doesn't guarantee production. If fruit is going to emerge, He must bring it, and He promises to do this only if we *abide* in Him.

So it is the task of the Vinedresser to lift it off the ground and place it on the trellis, where it will produce fruit again.[3]

Second, God prunes those branches that aren't bearing much or enough fruit. In his commentary on John, Merrill C. Tenney provides this helpful picture of the pruning process.

> In pruning a vine, two principles are generally observed: first, all dead wood must be ruthlessly removed; and second, the live wood must be cut back drastically. Dead wood harbors insects and disease and may cause the vine to rot, to say nothing of being unproductive and unsightly. Live wood must be trimmed back in order to prevent such heavy growth that the life of the vine goes into the wood rather than into fruit. The vineyards in the early spring look like a collection of barren, bleeding stumps; but in the fall they are filled with luxuriant purple grapes. As the farmer wields the pruning knife on his vines, so God cuts dead wood out from among His saints, and often cuts back the living wood so far that His method seems cruel. Nevertheless, from those who have suffered the most there often comes the greatest fruitfulness.[4]

Even though we've seen how beneficial the pruning process is, it is nevertheless a frightening prospect. Which is why in verse 3 we find Jesus pausing to assure His disciples that they are already properly prepared to bear fruit.

> "You are already clean because of the word which I have spoken to you." (John 15:3)

Through their faith and trust in Christ's Word, the disciples had already become clean, been justified before God, and been grafted into the Vine (see Rom. 5:1, 8–11). Their need for daily sanctifica-

---

3. "Theologians debate the unfruitful branch which is apparently cast away. . . . [The] probable solution is seen in the word *airei* (taketh away). This word is the root for *resurrection* (to take up). The focus here is fruitbearing; the vinedresser does not cut away a vine because it has no fruit but gently lifts it up to the sun so it has an opportunity to bear fruit." Elmer Towns, *The Gospel of John: Believe and Live* (Old Tappan, N.J.: Fleming H. Revell Co., 1990), pp. 273–74.

4. Merrill C. Tenney, *John: The Gospel of Belief* (Grand Rapids, Mich.: William B. Eerdmans Publishing Co., 1948), pp. 227–28.

tion and fruit bearing, however, still remained. And that is what Jesus made clear to them in John 15:4–5.

> "Abide in Me, and I in you. As the branch cannot bear fruit of itself, unless it abides in the vine, so neither can you, unless you abide in Me. I am the vine, you are the branches; he who abides in Me, and I in him, he bears much fruit; for apart from Me you can do nothing." (15:4–5)

What exactly does it mean to abide? It means to depend upon Him; to rely on, wait for, and draw strength from the Vine. Commentator William Barclay explains it this way:

> The secret of the life of Jesus was his contact with God; again and again he withdrew into a solitary place to meet him. We must keep contact with Jesus. We cannot do that unless we deliberately take steps to do it. To take but one example—to pray in the morning. . . . For most of us, it will mean a constant contact with him. It will mean arranging life, arranging prayer, arranging silence in such a way that there is never a day when we give ourselves a chance to forget him.[5]

It's extremely important that we cultivate Jesus' strategy for producing. We're commanded, on the one hand, to pursue Him— "Abide in Me"; and on the other, to wait for Him to produce fruit. If we don't abide in Him, Christ tells us the frank truth that "apart from Me you can do nothing." Author Ray Stedman helps us understand Jesus' words more fully.

> He does not mean that without him you remain just an immobile blob. You can operate your business without Christ. You can make it run well. You can raise your family without Christ. You can even pastor a church without Christ. But if you do, you will find that there will be no fruit, no Christlikeness, no manifestation of that beautiful character which arrests the attention of others. Instead there will be a

5. William Barclay, *The Gospel of John*, vol. 2, rev. ed., The Daily Study Bible Series (Philadelphia, Pa.: Westminster Press, 1975), p. 176.

sham, a phony imitation of the real thing, which will drive people away from Christ and will produce nothing but a dull, mechanical religiosity.[6]

Verse 6 lists an even more drastic consequence to living apart from Christ.

"If anyone does not abide in Me, he is thrown away as a branch, and dries up; and they gather them, and cast them into the fire, and they are burned."

Look carefully at Jesus' words: "If anyone does not abide in Me." Jesus isn't talking about a nonbeliever, for only a believer who is already *in* Christ can abide or not abide in Him. He's describing a Christian who is deliberately disobedient, someone who willfully follows the flesh instead of walking in the Spirit.[7] Such branches may be thrown out by the Vinedresser, cut off. They won't be torn from salvation, but their lives will be taken, which is also described in verse 6 as "dries up."[8]

Thus far, in the first half of verse 6, Jesus has used the singular *he* to refer to the branch. But notice in the second half, when it comes to the severity of judgment, He states everything in the plural. "They gather them . . . cast them . . . they are burned." "He" is thrown away, but "they" are cast in the fire. Meaning what? With the change to the plural, the focus moves away from the person and onto the fruits of that person's carnal life. The branch is cut off by divine discipline and the bitter fruits of the flesh that the branch was producing are burned up.

This same method of judgment is clearly described by the apostle Paul in 1 Corinthians 3.

For no man can lay a foundation other than the one which is laid, which is Jesus Christ. Now if any man builds upon the foundation with gold, silver, precious stones, wood, hay, straw, each man's work will become evident; for the day will show it, because it is to be revealed with fire; and the fire itself will test

6. Ray C. Stedman, *Expository Studies in John 13–17: Secrets of the Spirit*, A Discovery Bible Study Book (Waco, Tex.: Word Books, 1975), pp. 79–80.

7. The fruit of the flesh and the fruit of the Spirit are contrasted in Galatians 5:19–26.

8. Another example of the Lord taking the lives of disobedient believers is found in 1 Corinthians 11:23–34.

the quality of each man's work. If any man's work which he has built upon it remains, he shall receive a reward. If any man's work is burned up, he shall suffer loss; but he himself shall be saved, yet so as through fire. (vv. 11–15)

Picking back up with verse 7 in John 15, Jesus next explains four benefits for those who do abide in Him. First, our prayers will be answered.

"If you abide in Me, and My words abide in you, ask whatever you wish, and it shall be done for you."

Second, God is glorified.

"By this is My Father glorified, that you bear much fruit, and so prove to be My disciples." (v. 8)

Third, we'll be motivated by love.

"Just as the Father has loved Me, I have also loved you; abide in My love. If you keep My commandments, you will abide in My love; just as I have kept My Father's commandments, and abide in His love." (vv. 9–10)

And fourth, our joy will reach maximum expression.

"These things I have spoken to you, that My joy may be in you, and that your joy may be made full." (v. 11)

Practical Application of Jesus' Instruction

From our study of how to relate to the True Vine, two prominent principles emerge.

• *Refusal to abide is barrenness.* Don't chance it! Even though prideful independence may have its moments of pleasure and prosperity, a dry barrenness will remain in our inner souls and in our fruitless religion. Remember Proverbs 14:12:

There is a way which seems right to a man,
But its end is the way of death.

• *The result of abiding is fruitfulness.* Don't miss it! Composer Don Wyrtzen captures the truth of this in his personal lyric, "Psalm of My Life."

59

Like worthless chaff the wind blows away,
  Scorched by the bright desert sun through the
    day,
No root below, no fruit borne above,
  My life was thirsting for rains of His love.

While roaming far away on my own,
  I stood with sinners with hearts cold like
    stone,
I sat with scoffing cynics at play,
  Until my life changed direction one day.

While meditating day and night,
  His Word brought pleasure and highest delight,
It quenched my thirst and nurtured my soul,
  It satisfied me and made my life whole.

Then, like a lovely, well-watered tree,
  Nourished by rivers that flow endlessly,
Weighed down with luscious fruit from His hand,
  My full life prospered for Him in the land.[9]

-------------◆-------------

Father,

  I know the gnawing regret that comes from wasting many an hour, many a day operating in the flesh. It pierces me to think that none of those hours and days were motivated by a love for You. That none of them will bring You glory.

  Thank You, Vinedresser, for pruning, cleansing, lifting me up from the soil so that I can become laden with Your Son's holy fruit. Flow through me, True Vine; let Your love, patience, gentleness, and self-control burst forth in ripening acts of Christlikeness.

  Because of You, may my thoughts be cleaner, my motives purer, and my actions be glorifying, regardless of the outcome.

  I pray in the name of the True Vine. Amen.

9. Don Wyrtzen, "Psalm of My Life" © 1975 by Singspiration Music. All rights reserved. Used by permission. As quoted in *A Musician Looks at the Psalms,* by Don Wyrtzen (Grand Rapids, Mich.: Zondervan Publishing House, 1991), p. 21.

In the opening chapter of his book *Abide in Christ,* author Andrew Murray takes us back to when we first came to know Christ as our Savior.

> You doubtless have never repented having come at His call. You experienced that His word was truth; all His promises He fulfilled; He made you partakers of the blessings and the joy of His love. Was not His welcome most hearty, His pardon full and free, His love most sweet and precious? You more than once, at your first coming to Him, had reason to say, "The half was not told me."
>
> And yet you have had to complain of disappointment: as time went on, your expectations were not realized. The blessings you once enjoyed were lost; the love and joy of your first meeting with your Saviour, instead of deepening, have become faint and feeble. And often you have wondered what the reason could be, that with such a Saviour, so mighty and so loving, your experience of salvation should not have been a fuller one.[10]

Does this describe you? Is Jesus' reality only a faint shadow, a dim memory of what it used to be? Have you felt like complaining of disappointment? Are you wondering what's become of the closeness and passion you once enjoyed with Jesus?

Perhaps the root of this barrenness is a lack of communion with Christ.

Using the space provided, write down the ways in which you are currently communing with Him; not what you wish you were doing or are planning to do, just what you *are* doing. Let your focus be strictly on the time you and He spend together alone on a regular basis. Be unflinchingly honest.

---

10. Andrew Murray, *Abide in Christ* (Springdale, Pa.: Whitaker House, 1979), p. 11.

Have you found the source of your barrenness? Chances are, many of us will not even bother to fill in the space because there's nothing significant for us to put down. We're guilty of having left our first love, Jesus (Rev. 2:1–5). Oh, we know hymns, Scripture passages, and a lot of spiritual-sounding words. But we may have replaced the real fruit that comes from abiding in Him with the imitation fruit of religious activities. And that's not very satisfying.

If this has happened to you, and Jesus seems less and less real to you, let the next Living Insight be a new beginning, a fresh start of abiding in the True Vine.

Living Insights   STUDY TWO

Come, let's abide in the True Vine through worship centered on the fruits that flow from His very nature. Pause now to praise Him for His love, joy, peace, patience, kindness, goodness, faithfulness, gentleness, and self-control. To do this, slowly meditate on each one, savoring each redolent fruit of the Vine. See if there are any Scriptures that come to mind that express or illustrate each one. Gaze for as long as you can, then let your praises flow.

_____

_____

_____

_____

_____

Next, is there a specific time or event in your life when you can remember seeing Jesus' love? Have you felt His joy, experienced His kindness and goodness? As memories come to mind, offer up your heartfelt thanksgiving.

> I will give thanks to the Lord with all my heart;
> I will tell of all Thy wonders.
> I will be glad and exult in Thee;
> I will sing praise to Thy name, O Most High.
> (Ps. 9:1)

Journal

_____

_____

_____

_____

_____

_____

_____

_____

_____

_____

_____

_____

_____

_____

_____

_____

_____

Chapter 8
THE SHEPHERD
OF THE SHEEP
Selected Scriptures

"And what kind of animal would you like to be?" It's interesting that whenever a group of children are asked that question you practically never hear one of them shout, "A sheep!" Instead, you hear answers like, "A roaring lion" or, "A tall giraffe" or, "A huge elephant with great big tusks!"

Even the nations of the world have their favorite animals, and the sheep isn't one of them. There's the United States' eagle, China's panda, and Great Britain's lion. But no country wants a sheep for its national symbol.

And yet, somehow, many Christians have this romantic notion that being called a sheep is a compliment. Some of us are pleased to be known as sheep; we covet the association as if it were some kind of spiritual badge. If, however, we had ever spent time around a flock of sheep, we would quickly realize that there is nothing romantic or complimentary about being called one. And here are just a few reasons why.

A Few Realistic Thoughts on Sheep

First, to put it bluntly, sheep are stupid and stubborn. Ask yourself, have you ever seen a group of trained sheep in a circus? Now don't laugh. Have you? Of course not. You've seen trained dogs, seals, tigers, horses, even elephants, but no sheep. And you probably never will, because they're just too simpleminded.

Second, sheep are dirty and wayward. Real sheep aren't like those clean, fluffy balls of cotton depicted on cards. And if you've ever seen the southern end of a northbound herd, you'll know why. They can't keep themselves clean, and they smell atrocious. Plus, they tend to wander off easily. And no matter how many times you bring them back, they're prone to wander away again because they don't learn from their mistakes.

Third, sheep are defenseless and dependent. They are top-heavy; their legs are spindly; they are not fast, have no camouflage, and haven't much of a bite. Definitely not your king-of-the-forest types.

And fourth, sheep are easily frightened and confused. It doesn't take much to scramble the simple mental yolk of a nervous sheep. They've even been known to plunge straight over the edge of a high precipice in a panic, one following right after another.

Individually and collectively, these four unflattering facts point to one important truth: *Sheep need a shepherd.* And though it may not be a compliment to be called sheep—to know that we're sinfully stubborn, wayward, and foolish—it is comforting to know that we have a Shepherd, Jesus. Let's follow Him through the Scriptures now and find out more about this Guardian who protects and provides for such defenseless and dependent sheep as we.

A Threefold View of the Shepherd

The first New Testament passage we'll look at is John 10.

"Good Shepherd"

Beginning in verse 1, Jesus depicts a familiar scene to His listeners, that of a shepherd entering a sheepfold to gather his flock.

> "Truly, truly, I say to you, he who does not enter
> by the door into the fold of the sheep, but climbs
> up some other way, he is a thief and a robber. But
> he who enters by the door is a shepherd of the sheep.
> To him the doorkeeper opens, and the sheep hear
> his voice, and he calls his own sheep by name, and
> leads them out." (vv. 1–3)

Unlike many countries today, first-century Palestine raised sheep not to be killed for food but to produce wool and milk. This meant that the shepherd and sheep were together for years, allowing a bond to develop; a bond so strong that shepherds even named each of their sheep.

In addition to knowing each sheep by name, the shepherd provided leadership by going before his flock.

> "When he puts forth all his own, he goes before
> them, and the sheep follow him because they know
> his voice." (v. 4)

As the sheep heard the familiar sound of their shepherd's voice, they would follow him through the gate and out to pasture. He always went before them, and the sheep trusted him implicitly to guide them on the right paths.

With these familiar, everyday pictures, Jesus opens a window to the eternal for His disciples.

> "I am the good shepherd; the good shepherd lays down His life for the sheep." (v. 11)[1]

As our Good Shepherd, Jesus not only knows us by name and goes before us to lead, He also protects. He is a sacrificial shepherd, One who places Himself between His sheep and any attackers. In contrast to such courage and commitment is the cowardice of the hireling, a hired hand whose only concern is his wages.

> "He who is a hireling, and not a shepherd, who is not the owner of the sheep, beholds the wolf coming, and leaves the sheep, and flees, and the wolf snatches them, and scatters them. He flees because he is a hireling, and is not concerned about the sheep." (vv. 12–13)

Commentator William Barclay provides this helpful insight into the difference between a shepherd and a hireling.

> A real shepherd was born to his task. He was sent out with the flock as soon as he was old enough to go; the sheep became his friends and his companions; and it became second nature to think of them before he thought of himself. But the false shepherd came into the job, not as a calling, but as a means of making money. He was in it simply and solely for the pay he could get. He might even be a man who had taken to the hills because the town was too hot to hold him. He had no sense of the height and the responsibility of his task; he was only a hireling.[2]

---

1. The Greek word for "good" is *kalos,* which means that Jesus was not only good, but "that in the goodness there is a quality of winsomeness which makes it lovely. . . . In him there is more than efficiency and more than fidelity; there is loveliness. Sometimes in a village or town people speak about *the good doctor.* They are not thinking only of the doctor's efficiency and skill as a physician; they are thinking of the sympathy and the kindness and the graciousness which he brought with him and which made him the friend of all. In the picture of Jesus as the Good Shepherd there is loveliness as well as strength and power." William Barclay, *The Gospel of John,* vol. 2, rev. ed., The Daily Study Bible Series (Philadelphia, Pa.: Westminster Press, 1975), p. 62.

2. Barclay, *The Gospel of John,* vol. 2, p. 61.

Unlike the unfaithful hireling, Jesus' motivation for shepherding us is love, not selfish gain (compare v. 11 with 15:13).

"Great Shepherd"

The second passage where Jesus is referred to as our shepherd is found in the closing benediction to the book of Hebrews.

> Now the God of peace, who brought up from the dead the great Shepherd of the sheep through the blood of the eternal covenant, even Jesus our Lord, equip you in every good thing to do His will, working in us that which is pleasing in His sight, through Jesus Christ, to whom be the glory forever and ever. Amen. (Heb. 13:20–21)

The Great Shepherd who has been brought up from the dead is a clear reference to Jesus' resurrection. Having laid down His life for His sheep, He is pictured here, not as a mighty king returning to conquer foes, but as a compassionate shepherd come to lead His flock into good works that are pleasing to His Father.

But what if we wander from the works that please Him? Who will seek us out to bring us back into the fold? The same Great Shepherd who is also known as the Guardian of our souls.

> For you were continually straying like sheep, but now you have returned to the Shepherd and Guardian of your souls. (1 Peter 2:25)

"Chief Shepherd"

In the final passage of our study, 1 Peter 5, the Apostle describes Jesus as the "Chief Shepherd."

> Therefore, I exhort the elders among you, as your fellow elder and witness of the sufferings of Christ, and a partaker also of the glory that is to be revealed, shepherd the flock of God among you, exercising oversight not under compulsion, but voluntarily, according to the will of God; and not for sordid gain, but with eagerness; nor yet as lording it over those allotted to your charge, but proving to be examples to the flock. And when the Chief Shepherd appears, you will receive the unfading crown of glory. (vv. 1–4)

Interestingly, this section of Scripture is addressed to shepherds—elders, pastors, disciplers, small group Bible study leaders—people who lead flocks. People who must exercise great skill, patience, and grace in leading, not lording. For as Peter states, they are to be "among" their flock, not over them. To do this, to lead and not lord, the Apostle's first counsel is to shepherd God's people. A flock must be shepherded, not driven. You don't drive sheep, you drive cattle. A true shepherd will go before the flock instead of following behind it with a prod. Nor will he strike the sheep with caustic words as if they were racehorses needing to be whipped to do their best. Shepherding involves going before, setting an example for the rest to follow.

From Peter's earnest words we can draw out three rules for shepherding God's flock correctly.

- *Not under compulsion, but voluntarily.* True shepherds don't have to be forced into service. They want to minister, to help guide and equip others for their Chief Shepherd.

- *Not for sordid gain, but with eagerness.* The New International Version says, "not greedy for money." When money becomes more important than ministry, a leader crosses the boundary from being a shepherd to being a hireling.

- *Not abusing authority, but as servants.* Never once does the passage say that the flock belongs to the shepherd to do with as he or she pleases. It's the Lord's flock. Shepherd and sheep alike must submit to the Chief Shepherd. He is the One who promises us a reward if our work is done voluntarily, with eagerness and authenticity.

On Trusting Our Shepherd's Leadership

It may not be a compliment to be called sheep, but it is comforting to know that we have a Good Shepherd who calls us by name, who goes before us to guide and protect. So if He is leading, risk following. For He never leads down the wrong paths.

It's also wonderful to know that we have a Great Shepherd who equips us for service and seeks us when we stray. So if He's calling, return to the fold. He will not abandon His wandering sheep.

And it's exciting to know that we have a Chief Shepherd who will not overlook any deed deserving of reward. So if He's being glorified, relax and enjoy.

---◆---

Great Shepherd,

How could I ever doubt Your love? Why am I afraid to follow? Forgive me, Lord, for truly I am foolish and stubborn. Time and again I have wandered far from Your righteous path. Still, You come. You rescue me because of the great love with which You love me—ME— a sheep!

Teach me, Jesus, to come at Your call, to obey and not kick against Your correcting staff. Draw me close, let me know the comfort of Your vigilant care. Be my defense in danger. For I am Your sheep, defenseless and dependent, and I need a shepherd. I need You, Jesus, Good Shepherd of my soul. Amen.

Living Insights

When Phillip Keller talks about shepherding, he's not simply repeating something he read in *National Geographic*; he's speaking from firsthand experience. Such is the story you're about to read, a story prompted by Psalm 23:1.

> The Lord is my Shepherd,
> I shall not want.

When all is said and done the welfare of any flock is entirely dependent upon the management afforded them by their owner.

The tenant sheepman on the farm next to my first ranch was the most indifferent manager I had ever met. He was not concerned about the condition of his sheep. His land was neglected. He gave little or no time to his flock, letting them pretty well forage for themselves as best they could, both summer and winter. They fell prey to dogs, cougars and rustlers.

Every year these poor creatures were forced to gnaw away at bare brown fields and impoverished pastures. Every winter there was a shortage of nourishing hay and wholesome grain to feed the hungry ewes. Shelter to safeguard and protect the suffering sheep from storms and blizzards was scanty and inadequate.

They had only polluted, muddy water to drink. There had been a lack of salt and other trace minerals needed to offset their sickly pastures. In their thin, weak and diseased condition these poor sheep were a pathetic sight.

In my mind's eye I can still see them standing at the fence, huddled sadly in little knots, staring wistfully through the wires at the rich pastures on the other side.

To all their distress, the heartless, selfish owner seemed utterly callous and indifferent. He simply did not care. What if his sheep did *want* green grass; fresh water; shade; safety or shelter from the storms? What if they did *want* relief from wounds, bruises, disease and parasites?

He ignored their needs—he couldn't care less. Why should he—they were just sheep—fit only for the slaughterhouse.

I never looked at those poor sheep without an acute awareness that this was a precise picture of those wretched old taskmasters, Sin and Satan, on their derelict ranch—scoffing at the plight of those within their power.[3]

In light of the calloused care of sin and Satan, have you ever really stopped to consider just how good the Good Shepherd is to you? How well He provides? How concerned He is about your safety?

Take some time to go through the following verses, and write down all the wonderful traits of the Great Shepherd that you see: Psalm 25:8–15; 84:11–12; 145:8–21; Isaiah 40:11. Next, think back on the specific ways that He has provided for you personally, and note any new traits of the Shepherd that are revealed.

_____

_____

_____

3. Phillip Keller, A Shepherd Looks at Psalm 23 (Grand Rapids, Mich.: Zondervan Publishing House, Daybreak Books, 1970), pp. 28–29.

Finally, drawing upon your notes and experience, write a composite word picture of the Good Shepherd.

_____

_____

_____

_____

_____

_____

_____

_____

_____

🍇 *Living Insights* STUDY TWO

In his *Historical Geography of the Holy Land,* Sir George Adam Smith wrote:

> With us sheep are often left to themselves; but I do not remember ever to have seen in the East a flock of sheep without a shepherd. In such a landscape as Judaea, where a day's pasture is thinly scattered over an unfenced tract of country, covered with delusive paths, still frequented by wild beasts, and rolling off into the desert, the man and his character are indispensable. On some high moor, across which at night the hyaenas howl, when you meet him, sleepless, far-sighted, weather-beaten, armed, leaning on his staff, and looking out over his scattered sheep, everyone of them on his heart, you understand why the shepherd of Judaea sprang to the forefront of his people's history; why they gave his name to their

71

king, and made him the symbol of providence; why
Christ took him as the type of self-sacrifice.[4]

Just imagine for a moment . . . can you see Jesus, sleepless,
farsighted, weather-beaten, armed, leaning on His staff, looking
out over His sheep, every one of them on His heart—including you?

Why not set aside the whole day to dwell on this picture and
praise Him for what it reveals. For example, His unceasing care for
you night and day (Ps. 121), His self-sacrificing love (Phil. 2:3–8),
His . . . what? Keep going!

Journal

_____

_____

_____

_____

_____

_____

_____

_____

_____

_____

_____

_____

4. As quoted by William Barclay in _Jesus as They Saw Him_ (1962; reprint, Grand Rapids,
Mich.: William B. Eerdmans Publishing Co., 1980), pp. 198–99.

Chapter 9

THE LAMB OF GOD
Selected Scriptures

If God were to suddenly appear on earth today, we would expect Him to come in power—healing the sick, raising the dead, and calming nature's tempests. But we wouldn't expect that power to reside in someone meek and humble. We would expect Him to come like a lion, not like a lamb.

But like a lamb is the way Jesus came, gentle and humble in heart (Matt. 11:29), seating a child on His lap, riding a lowly donkey instead of a chariot, and eating with society's outcasts instead of with heads of state.

Temperament is only one way in which Jesus was like a lamb, however. We'll see many more of His lamblike qualities if we study lambs, especially through the lens of Scripture.

Lambs throughout Scripture

Looking back at the Old Testament era, we'll find that lambs held an important sacrificial role in Israel's history.

Old Testament

Remember how God tested Abraham by commanding him to offer his only son as a burnt offering? The aged patriarch obeyed God, arising the next morning to take Isaac to Mount Moriah. When their destination was within sight,

> Abraham said to his young men, "Stay here with the donkey, and I and the lad will go yonder; and we will worship and return to you." And Abraham took the wood of the burnt offering and laid it on Isaac his son, and he took in his hand the fire and the knife. So the two of them walked on together. And Isaac spoke to Abraham his father and said, "My father!" And he said, "Here I am, my son." And he said, "Behold, the fire and the wood, but where is the lamb for the burnt offering?" (Gen. 22:5–7)

Isaac was old enough to understand that they were going to offer a sacrifice to the Lord. And you can see by his response that lambs were commonly used for such occasions. For instead of asking, "Where's the sacrifice?" he specifically asked, "Where's the lamb?" If you read on, you'll see that God actually did provide Abraham with a sheep to sacrifice in the place of his son.

Turning to Exodus 29, we find the lamb referred to again as a sacrifice in the Lord's instructions to Israel concerning the daily burnt offering.

> "Now this is what you shall offer on the altar: two one year old lambs each day, continuously. The one lamb you shall offer in the morning, and the other lamb you shall offer at twilight." (vv. 38–39)

Can you imagine? That's 14 lambs a week, 56 a month, 672 a year! And that's just for this one offering. There were many, many more (see Lev. 14:10; 23:18–20).[1]

Lambs were also sacrificed during the worship celebrations the Lord established for the Jews in Leviticus 23.

> Then the Lord spoke to Moses, saying, "Speak to the sons of Israel, and say to them, 'When you enter the land which I am going to give to you and reap its harvest, then you shall bring in the sheaf of the first fruits of your harvest to the priest. And he shall wave the sheaf before the Lord for you to be accepted; on the day after the sabbath the priest shall wave it. Now on the day when you wave the sheaf, you shall offer a male lamb one year old without defect for a burnt offering to the Lord.'" (vv. 9–12)

Over in 1 Chronicles 29, we find David exulting in all the preparations for the building of the Lord's temple. By themselves, David and the leaders of Israel had donated more than 46,610 tons of gold, silver, and bronze for its construction.[2] All of Israel rejoiced, and David offered up a prayer of dedication that was affirmed the

---

1. Another example is in Numbers 6, where we are told that if a man or woman who has taken the Nazirite vow of dedication to the Lord becomes defiled, a lamb must be sacrificed as a guilt offering (vv. 1–12).

2. Eugene H. Merrill, "1 Chronicles," in *The Bible Knowledge Commentary*, Old Testament edition, ed. John F. Walvoord and Roy B. Zuck (Wheaton, Ill.: Scripture Press Publications, Victor Books, 1985), p. 616.

next day by a huge sacrifice that included a thousand lambs and a thousand rams (vv. 10–21).

But of all the scenes in the Old Testament involving a sacrifice, none carry more significance and symbolism than the story of the Passover lamb found in Exodus 12. After the children of Israel had spent four hundred years of slavery in Egypt, the Lord sent Moses to demand that Pharaoh release them. When Pharaoh stubbornly refused, God sent a plague upon Egypt. Pharaoh still refused, and Egypt suffered another plague, and another, and another. Finally, after nine plagues and nine refusals, God gave Moses instructions to pass along to the children of Israel so that they could protect themselves from the tenth and final plague. For God was about to send "the destroyer" to kill the firstborn of every person and animal in Egypt.

> Then Moses called for all the elders of Israel, and said to them, "Go and take for yourselves lambs according to your families, and slay the Passover lamb. And you shall take a bunch of hyssop and dip it in the blood which is in the basin, and apply some of the blood that is in the basin to the lintel and the two doorposts; and none of you shall go outside the door of his house until morning. For the Lord will pass through to smite the Egyptians; and when He sees the blood on the lintel and on the two doorposts, the Lord will pass over the door and will not allow the destroyer to come in to your houses to smite you. And you shall observe this event as an ordinance for you and your children forever." (vv. 21–24)

God wanted Israel to remember that night. He wanted them to remember Him as their Deliverer and to remember that it was the blood of the sacrificial lamb that protected them from the destroyer. For this was to be an object lesson preparing the people for the coming Messiah, whose blood would be shed as a sacrifice for their sins.

And the people did remember. As one historian points out, Passover became ingrained in the life of every Jew.

> The Passover Feast stood at the very heart of Jewish life and religion. Every adult male Jew who lived within twenty miles of Jerusalem was bound by law to attend it, and it was the ambition of every devout Jew who lived outside Palestine to attend at least

one Passover Feast in Jerusalem, even if he had to save for half a lifetime to do so.[3]

New Testament

During the time of Christ, the system of sacrifices established in the Old Testament era were still being faithfully practiced. For example, in Mark 14:12–15, we find Jesus and the disciples making plans to observe the Passover Feast. Little did the disciples realize that as they were preparing their Passover, God was preparing a Passover of His own. Not with a literal lamb, but with His Son, Jesus, the Lamb of God.

Like that first unblemished Passover lamb, the sinless Son of God was sacrificed the next day on Passover. His blood was shed on the crossbeams of a crucifix to deliver us from bondage to sin.

In his book *Jesus as They Saw Him*, author William Barclay insightfully reveals the parallels between the Passover lamb and Jesus, the Lamb of God.

The Passover Lamb stood for two things.

The Passover lamb was the symbol of deliverance. Nowhere in history did the Jews see the delivering power of God so clearly and definitely demonstrated as in the events which brought them out of Egypt. Here was the deliverance *par excellence*, and without parallel. And to think of Jesus as the Passover lamb is to see in him the delivering and rescuing power of God come to earth for the salvation of men. Just as the first Passover lamb was the sign of God's deliverance of his people from their slavery in Egypt, so Jesus the second Passover lamb is the symbol of their deliverance from slavery to sin.

But there is a real sense in which the Passover lamb was more than a symbol of deliverance; it was *the means of deliverance*. It was the mark of the blood of the lamb, which the lamb had to die to provide, which was the means which kept the Jewish homes safe on that terrible night of death and destruction. The death of the lamb was essential for the deliverance

---

3. William Barclay, *Jesus as They Saw Him* (1962; reprint, Grand Rapids, Mich.: William B. Eerdmans Publishing Co., 1980), p. 305.

of the people. Jesus therefore is the means of salvation whereby men are saved from the penalty and the power of their sins. Through his sacrifice and death that salvation came.[4]

Looking back, decades after Christ's death, the apostle Paul affirmed this view of Christ when he wrote, "For Christ our Passover also has been sacrificed" (1 Cor. 5:7b).

God's Lamb on Earth

Just as the Passover prefigured Christ's death, we find a similar pattern of prophecy and fulfillment when we compare Isaiah 53 with Acts 8.

Biblical References

Centuries before the birth of Christ, the prophet Isaiah foretold of a suffering servant who, like a sacrificial lamb, would be "pierced through for our transgressions" (v. 5). Picking up in verse 7, we read,

> He was oppressed and He was afflicted,
> Yet He did not open His mouth;
> Like a lamb that is led to slaughter,
> And like a sheep that is silent before its shearers,
> So He did not open His mouth.

Who was Isaiah speaking of? In Acts 8, we're told that this same question puzzled an Ethiopian official who was reading Isaiah's prophecy as he traveled home from a pilgrimage to Jerusalem. It was then that Philip, one of Jesus' disciples, came alongside the man's chariot and asked,

> "Do you understand what you are reading?" And he said, "Well, how could I, unless someone guides me?" And he invited Philip to come up and sit with him. Now the passage of Scripture which he was reading was this:
> "He was led as a sheep to slaughter;
> And as a lamb before its shearer is silent,
> So He does not open His mouth.
> In humiliation His judgment was taken away;

---

4. Barclay, *Jesus as They Saw Him*, pp. 305–6.

Who shall relate His generation?
For His life is removed from the earth."
And the eunuch answered Philip and said, "Please
tell me, of whom does the prophet say this? Of himself, or of someone else?" And Philip opened his
mouth, and beginning from this Scripture he preached
Jesus to him. (vv. 30b–35)

From prophecy to fulfillment, let's turn now to a final passage
in 1 Peter 1, where, again, we find one of the Apostles looking
back and affirming Jesus as the Lamb of God.

And if you address as Father the One who impar-
tially judges according to each man's work, conduct
yourselves in fear during the time of your stay upon
earth; knowing that you were not redeemed with
perishable things like silver or gold from your futile
way of life inherited from your forefathers, but with
precious blood, as of a lamb unblemished and spot-
less, the blood of Christ. (vv. 17–19)[5]

Symbolic Meanings

As we look back at the varied and vivid portraits of the lamb
in Scripture, at least four symbolic meanings become clear. First,
the lamb symbolizes sacrifice. Second, it represents dependence.
Third, it personifies innocence. And fourth, it signifies the combined qualities of meekness, gentleness, and humility.

Qualities of a Lamb Worth Emulating

Drawing from the symbolic meanings portrayed by the lamb in
Scripture, here are four qualities for every believer to emulate.

Life of dependence. No lamb even looks like it can make it on
its own. It is a totally dependent creature, just as we are. Like a
lamb that constantly stays by its shepherd's side, we, too, must
constantly stay by our Lord's side.

Trust in the Lord with all your heart,
And do not lean on your own understanding.

5. For further study of Christ as the Lamb in the New Testament, read Revelation 5:1–14;
12:10–11; 19:7–9; 21:22–23.

In all your ways acknowledge Him,
And He will make your paths straight.
(Prov. 3:5–6)

Presence of approachability. No one is afraid to approach a lamb. There is a meekness and gentleness about it that is attractive and inviting. Could that same thing be said about you? Are you cultivating a nature that is "gentle and humble in heart," like Christ's (Matt. 11:29)?

Heart of innocence. Isn't it refreshing to meet people today who are still innocent as lambs? People who posses a simple purity that is a joy to be around? We can be like that, if we'll remember Paul's advice:

Do all things without grumbling or disputing; that you may prove yourselves to be blameless and innocent, children of God above reproach in the midst of a crooked and perverse generation, among whom you appear as lights in the world. (Phil. 2:14–15)

Spirit of sacrifice. Do you possess a lamblike spirit of sacrifice? Are you willing to lay down your life, your rights, your time, your talents—everything—for the One who laid it all down for you?

And He died for all, that they who live should no longer live for themselves, but for Him who died and rose again on their behalf. (2 Cor. 5:15)

◆

O Lord,

*Worthy is the Lamb that was slain
to receive power and riches
wisdom and might
honor, glory, and blessing.*

*To You, O Lord, and to the Lamb,
be blessing and honor and glory and dominion
forever and ever.
Amen.*[6]

6. Prayer taken from Revelation 5:12–13.

Have you ever celebrated a Passover? Though space won't allow a more detailed explanation, we've set aside the next two Living Insights for Zola Levitt, a Hebrew Christian, to lead you through the highlights of a Passover meal from a Christian perspective. In doing so, it is our hope that you'll "gain a marvelous insight into the very essence of Christianity—the sacrifice of the Lamb."[7]

> **Purge out the leaven.** Passover doesn't just happen. It takes a lot of preparation.
>
> The house must be clean—sterilized—in honor of this great occasion. Every family member participates in this one-of-a-kind housecleaning.
>
> Particularly, the house must be free of all leaven. Leaven is simply yeast, the stuff that makes bread rise, and it's found in bread, cake, cookies and so forth. In the Bible leaven is symbolic of sin.
>
> Father plays a game with the children concerning getting out the leaven. While mother is busy in the kitchen, bringing out the special Passover dishes and tableware, father hides crumbs of bread throughout the house—on the bookshelves, behind the furniture, on window sills. Then the children come like an army, ferreting out all the crumbs. When they find some leaven they shout for father, who comes with a feather and a wooden spoon. He carefully brushes the crumbs into the spoon with the feather, carries them to the fire and throws them in. Thus all those little sins and bad works are burned up ("And the fire shall try every man's work of what sort it is." 1 Cor. 3:13).
>
> . . . Paul alludes to this symbol: "Purge out therefore the old leaven, that ye may be a new lump, as ye are unleavened. For even *Christ our Passover* is sacrificed for us: Therefore let us keep the feast, not with the old leaven, neither with the leaven of malice and wickedness; but with the unleavened bread of sincerity and truth" (1 Cor. 5:7–8). . . .

7. Zola Levitt, *The Miracle of Passover* (Dallas, Tex.: Zola Levitt, 1977), p. 3. (See Zola Levitt Ministries, Box 12268, Dallas, Texas 75225).

White linen, the righteousness of saints. White linen is symbolic of righteousness in the Scriptures (Rev. 19:7–8), and the cleansed home is trimmed with it for the service. The table is set with a white table-cloth and white candles, and father dons a white robe, called a *kittel,* and a white crown. . . .

The splendid white artifacts . . . lend an atmosphere of purity and festivity to the meal. Father's costume is that of the High Priest in the Tabernacle, who wore a pure white robe, and the effect is that part of the official Temple worship has been brought home for Passover. Father also symbolizes the risen Christ, the High Priest. . . .

For women only. Now the candles are lit, as the preparation continues. Interestingly they are lit by a woman. . . .

. . . The mother of the house is supposed to do it.

The symbol there is obvious. It was a woman who brought us Christ, the light of the world. . . .

The first cup. Four cups of wine will be drunk as part of the Passover festivities. The first cup is called the Cup of Sanctification, and it simply sanctifies the table and all of the preparations. Note that the service has still not begun—everything is still being made ready. . . .

The hidden bread. After the first cup the father takes three loaves of the unleavened bread and places them in a special white linen envelope which has three compartments. A "loaf" of unleavened bread looks like a big soda cracker, rather than what we now think of as a loaf. . . .

In a special ceremony of his own, father removes the *middle* loaf from its compartment, breaks it, wraps it in a separate piece of white linen and hides it away. He "buries" it behind the cushion on his chair. . . .

The four questions. Now the youngest member of the family who can read asks Father the Four Questions. . . .

The questions are very general and give father a chance to hold forth with the whole story of the Exodus:

1. Why is this night distinguished from all other nights? On this night we eat only unleavened bread.
2. On all other nights we eat any kinds of herbs, but on this night only bitter herbs. Why?
3. On all other nights we do not dip, but tonight we dip twice. Why?
4. On this night we all recline in our chairs at the table. Why? . . .

. . . The unleavened bread symbolizes purity, of course, since leaven is sin. . . .

The bitter herbs remind us of the bitterness of slavery in Egypt. . . .

The dipping, by which Jesus identified his betrayer, Judas ("The one who dips after me"), has several traditional meanings. The one I always liked best concerned the traveling across the Red Sea on dry land. Since the parsley is dipped twice in salt water the image is most telling. The first dip is Israel, going into the Sea and coming out unharmed. The second dip is for the Egyptian army who tried to follow them—the parsley is dipped and then immediately eaten. Down the hatch with Pharaoh's persecutors! . . .

As to the fourth question—the reclining in the chairs—this has to do with freedom. The Jews are no longer slaves and so they can relax. . . .

The second cup. The second cup is spilled into the individual plates in front of each person, a drop at a time. . . .

Those ten red drops . . . are clearly representative of those terrible ten smitings of Egypt. The father somberly chants the name of each plague: "Blood . . . Frogs . . . Vermin . . . Beasts . . .".

The meal. The melancholy moment is dissipated quickly as the meal comes out. Mother has prepared quite a feast for the occasion. . . .

The meal is leisurely and joyful, much like a Thanksgiving or Christmas dinner. . . .

The third cup. Now comes the most beautiful and touchingly symbolic part of all—the third cup, which is The Cup of Redemption.

It is now time to bring forth that buried loaf of unleavened bread, which will serve as the dessert to the meal. The *afikomin*, as it is called . . . is sometimes recovered by a child. Father must redeem it in silver (I used to get a nickel . . .).

That buried unleavened bread—the middle piece! —is then eaten with the third cup of wine. . . .

Now let's examine this bread and wine more thoroughly.

Let's say, for the sake of argument, that the three loaves represent the Trinity, and that the middle one is the Son. It was *that* one, the Son in the Trinity, which we broke ("His body broken for you"); wrapped in white linen and buried, as was the body of Jesus; and now bring forth to eat with the *Cup of Redemption* (that is the *Jewish* term for this cup). Everyone must partake of it ("The bread of life") and it is the last thing eaten, as though the eating of *this* piece of bread will sustain everyone from here on.

In the actual ceremony Father breaks off pieces from this loaf . . . and passes the pieces around the table. Each person eats his piece and drinks the third cup with it. . . .

Now, before leaving the bread, we should point out how very like His body it really is. It has stripes ("By His stripes we are healed"); it's pierced ("They shall look upon Me Whom they have pierced"); and it's pure, containing no leaven (no sin). . . .

Let's look now at the wine.

That third cup has every bit as much significance as the bread. . . .

Matthew 26:27–28 records the Lord raising the Cup of Redemption:

> And He took the cup, *and gave thanks,* and
> gave it to them, saying, Drink ye all of it; For

83

this is my blood of the new testament, which
is shed for many for the remission of sins. . . .

To finish with the magnificent third cup of wine,
we need to consider Jesus' statement, "Do this in
remembrance of me." We are perfectly obedient to
that, of course, when we take communion, but the
statement should be realized in its fullness. . . .

Probably Jesus was saying this: "Brothers, you
have always kept Passover and it has helped to remind you that God delivered our people from Egypt.
But that was a type-symbol. I am the fulfillment of
that symbol. I can deliver you from this whole world.
So, when you do this from now on, don't do it so
much in remembrance of the Exodus, *Do this in remembrance of me*." . . .

The fourth cup. Jesus didn't drink the fourth cup,
and there's a good reason why He didn't.

The fourth cup—The Cup of Praise—is sometimes called Elijah's cup. It is at this point in the
Passover service that the Jews look for the literal
fulfillment of Mal. 4:5: "Behold, I will send you Elijah
the prophet before the coming of the great and
dreadful day of the Lord." . . .

Jesus and His men didn't partake of that cup
because the Messiah was already there, of course.
And Jesus had stated that John the Baptist had come
in the spirit of Elijah and had already announced
the Messiah.

The hymn. In the gospel it says, concluding the
Passover, "And when they had sung an hymn, they
went out into the Mount of Olives" (Mt. 26:30).

My family did better than that. We didn't sing
just one hymn—we sang eight or ten! And I mean
we *really sang!*

. . . We gave Passover a send-off that would
last a whole year![8]

8. Levitt, *The Miracle of Passover*, pp. 6–11, 13, 15–17, 18, 20, 26–27, 29.

For worship, why not celebrate a communion with your family, incorporating some of these highlights of a Passover? It's full of rich meanings and wonderful ritual; something that could perhaps become a family tradition. What a wonderful way to teach your children about the Lamb of God!

Journal

Chapter 10

THE WAY, THE TRUTH, THE LIFE
John 14:1–6

John 14 is a chapter for those who have heart trouble. Not an actual physical problem, mind you, but the kind of inner *disease* that comes from the build up of high-cholesterol anxieties in our hearts.

All of us are susceptible to troubled hearts; it's a very common human condition. And as we shall see in our lesson, the disciples were certainly no exception. They were, however, offered a cure, one that's still available today. It doesn't come in the form of a liquid or a pill but, surprisingly, in a person—Jesus.

So let's step inside John's gospel and find out not only what ailed the disciples, but also what name Jesus prescribed as a remedy for their troubled hearts.

The Biblical Backdrop

First, it would help if we briefly examined the disciples' medical history coming into this lesson's passage. Did any of them have thyroid problems? No. Diabetes? No. Had they heard any disturbing news recently that might cause deep feelings of anxiety or fear about the future? *Yes.*

When It Was Spoken

The disciples heard this distressing news the night before Jesus was crucified. They were celebrating Passover together when the Master stunned them with the unexpected announcement that one of them would betray Him (John 13:21). A second blow quickly followed when Jesus said He would be with them only a little while longer and that where He was going they could not come (v. 33). And last, they were shaken by the depressing news that one of them, a leader, would soon deny their Lord (vv. 36–38).

The disciples were dumbfounded. Jesus—gone? How could their Master, Savior, leader, friend, the One for whom they had given up everything to follow, suddenly abandon them? None of this made sense; it was the exact opposite of anything they had expected.

John's heart was racing; Peter felt a searing chest pain; James, as well as the rest of the disciples, felt a rising panic and shortness of breath.

Knowing that His words troubled His disciples' hearts deeply, Jesus immediately began to comfort them.

"Let not your heart be troubled." (14:1a)

The Greek term Christ used for *troubled* means "disturbed, frightened, stirred up." He put His finger right on the problem. Unfortunately, not everyone who needed His healing touch was there to receive it.

To Whom It Was Said

Only eleven disciples heard Jesus' initial words of comfort; for Judas, the betrayer, had already departed (13:21–30).

So the Lord exhorted the rest to keep on believing.

"Believe in God, believe also in Me." (14:1b)

In essence, Jesus was saying, "You believed in Me before I gave you this distressing news; keep on believing in Me now. Don't stop!" And to help strengthen their foundering hearts, He pulled back the curtains on some wonderful future events.

"In My Father's house are many dwelling places; if it were not so, I would have told you; for I go to prepare a place for you. And if I go and prepare a place for you, I will come again, and receive you to Myself; that where I am, there you may be also." (vv. 2–3)

Jesus knew that He was about to die, but He assured the disciples that He would live on to be with His Father and that they would one day be with Him again. He also left them with the bright promise that He would personally return to take them to the eternal dwelling place He would prepare for them in His Father's house.

As hopeful as that picture of the future was, Jesus could see in the disciples' eyes that they were still anxious about the present. Fear was causing them to become disoriented in their thinking, to forget the things He had taught them. So, He offered them the simple reminder,

"And you know the way where I am going." (v. 4)

To the great relief, no doubt, of the other bewildered disciples, Thomas blurted out,

> "Lord, we do not know where You are going, how do we know the way?" (v. 5)

You can almost hear the hysteria, the frustration in his voice. "Wait! Hold on, Jesus. I don't get it—none of us are getting it. Way? What way? What are You talking about?"

In response, Jesus graciously revealed one of the most comprehensive of all His names; a name potent enough to calm the most troubled heart.

> Jesus said to him, "I am the way, and the truth, and the life; no one comes to the Father, but through Me." (v. 6)

A Verbal Analysis

Let's look carefully at the three different components combined in this one name. For, as we shall see, each one carries a different meaning and produces a different effect in those who receive it by faith.

"The Way"

Hidden within this Greek term for *way*, which means "path" or "road," is the idea of a journey, of going from one point to another. Jesus is saying that *He* is the way to eternal life with God, the bridge that spans the gap between sinful humanity and holy divinity.

As you look through Scripture, you'll find the "way" being mentioned again and again. For example, in Psalm 27:11, David prayed, "Teach me Thy way, O Lord." In Deuteronomy 5:32–33, Israel is told to "walk in all the way which the Lord your God has commanded you." In Isaiah 30:21, the prophet heard God say, "This is the way, walk in it." In Matthew 22:16, the Pharisees' disciples addressed Jesus as one who "teach[es] the way of God in truth." Over in 2 Peter 2:21, the Apostle warns against knowing the way of righteousness but not walking in it. And in Acts 9:2 and 19:9, when Christianity was first named, it was even called "the Way."

Even outside the Scriptures we have examples such as Philo, who called philosophy "The Royal Way"; and Confucius, who named his teaching, "Tao," the way.[1] But, as William Barclay points out,

> the claim of Jesus goes beyond any of these sayings, great as they are. Jesus did not say: "I show you the way." He did not even say: "I open for you the way." He said: "I *am* the way." Let us take a human analogy. We may direct a person to his destination in words, giving him careful and detailed instructions as to how to get there. We may supply a person with a map which gives him his route and with a careful description of it. But even with the most careful instructions and even with the best of maps a person may still get lost. Best of all is to say to the person: "I know the way, come with me, and I myself will take you there." Then the last possibility of losing the way is gone. For that person we then become the way. Even so Jesus did not only tell us the way; he did not only give instruction about the way; he *is* the way in whom no man can fail to find his way into the presence of God.[2]

"The Truth"

Probably no search has lasted longer and produced more incorrect answers than the search for truth. Commentator Merrill Tenney called truth "the scarcest commodity in the world," adding:

> All the philosophers had sought for it; none had attained it. . . . Truth is neither an abstract system of integrated propositions, nor is it an impersonal ethic contained in many rules. It is both the reality and the ethic expressed in a person.[3]

And that person in whom reality and ethic are perfectly expressed is Jesus, the paragon of truth.

The following discussion by Barclay regarding the word *truth* and its various shades of meaning provides us with an even richer understanding and appreciation of the word.

---

1. See William Barclay, *Jesus as They Saw Him* (1962; reprint, Grand Rapids, Mich.: William B. Eerdmans Publishing Co., 1980), pp. 278-79.

2. Barclay, *Jesus as They Saw Him*, p. 279.

3. Merrill C. Tenney, *John: The Gospel of Belief* (Grand Rapids, Mich.: William B. Eerdmans Publishing Co., 1948), p. 215.

In Hebrew, the word for *truth, emeth,* typically means, "fidelity, reliability, trustworthiness, faithfulness." When applied to Jesus, it means that He is "fidelity incarnate, that we can completely and unhesitatingly and without reservation rely on Him."[4]

In Greek, the word for truth, *alētheia,* has a double meaning. "It means *truth as distinguished from falsehood,* and it means that which is *real and genuine* as opposed to that which is *unreal and counterfeit."*[5]

And in the gospel of John, truth is "not simply something which is intellectual, it is also something which is moral; it is not something which is simply to be known, it is something which is also to be done."[6] In summary, Barclay writes,

> To say that Jesus is the Truth is at one and the same time to say that Jesus is the incarnation of fidelity, the revelation of reality, and the pattern of goodness.[7]

"The Life"

Let's again consider the thoughts of Merrill Tenney, as he skillfully weaves together the meaning of Christ's final attribute with the first two we've discussed.

> The way was a means of reaching the Father; the truth defined the righteous standards of the way; the life bespoke the dynamic which could make attainment possible. All through the Gospel of John *life* describes the principle of spiritual vitality that originates with God and that lifts men out of sin to Himself. . . . Christianity is not a system of philosophy, nor a ritual, nor a code of laws; it is the impartation of a divine vitality. Without the way there is no going, without the truth there is no knowing, without the life there is no living.[8]

4. Barclay, Jesus as *They Saw Him,* p. 279.
5. Barclay, Jesus as *They Saw Him,* p. 280.
6. Barclay, Jesus as *They Saw Him,* p. 280.
7. Barclay, Jesus as *They Saw Him,* p. 281.
8. Tenney, *John,* pp. 215–16.

The Practical Significance

For our troubled hearts to derive any practical benefit from Jesus' name "the Way, the Truth, and the Life," we must take it, taste it, let its various elements be digested into our beliefs and into the bloodstream of our inner thoughts.

Once there, the Way will relieve our fear of being or getting lost, because in Him we'll find direction, purpose, and assurance of the future. The Truth will remove our need to anxiously continue searching for the answers to life, because in Him we have the wisdom of God. And the Life will reinforce our hope for a home in heaven, because He has gone before to prepare us a place.

> *O Lord Jesus Christ, who art the Way, the Truth, and the Life, we pray thee suffer us not to stray from thee, who art the Way, nor to distrust thee, who art the Truth, nor to rest in any other thing than thee who art the Life. Teach us, by thy Holy Spirit, what to believe, what to do, and wherein to take our rest.* [9]

Amen.

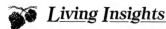

Living Insights

Is your heart troubled? Could it be, perhaps, that you've chosen to go your own way in life instead of following "the Way, the Truth, and the Life"? Proverbs 14:12 states,

> There is a way which seems right to a man,
> But its end is the way of death.

Jesus is the new and living way God has provided for your salvation (Heb. 10:19–20). Don't be misled by those who would tell you there are many paths to God. Jesus said, "I am *the* way, and *the* truth, and *the* life; no one comes to the Father, but through Me" (John 14:6, emphasis added). All other paths are detours that lead to nothing but dead ends.

---

9. Erasmus, as quoted by Barclay in *Jesus as They Saw Him*, p. 283.

But the Way is sure, and leads to a sure end—
eternal life through Jesus Christ, our Lord, our living
Way.[10]

🍇 *Living Insights*

Using our study as a springboard, spend some time now in praise
and thanksgiving. Focus on the wonderful insights into Jesus' character that you learned from His name "the Way, the Truth, and the
Life." Space has been provided for you to list the ones that are most
meaningful to you. Then, as new thoughts, insights, and cor-
relations come to mind during your prayer time, use your journal
to record your thoughts.

The Way _____

_____

The Truth _____

_____

The Life _____

_____

| Journal |

_____

_____

_____

_____

_____

_____

10. Mary Foxwell Loeks, *The Glorious Names of God* (Grand Rapids, Mich.: Baker Book
House, 1986), p. 32.

Chapter 11

CHRIST, OUR MEDIATOR
Selected Scriptures

"Excuse me, I believe that's mine."—"Sorry, I'm quite sure it's mine."
"But I *know* it belongs to me."——"Well, I'm afraid it doesn't."
"You're mistaken."———"No, *you* are."
"Give it back!"———"Not on your life."
"Thief."————"Lunatic!"

A few more testy words between these two and the breach will become—well, it already is—impassable. A line has been drawn that neither person will cross because they're too busy digging in, stubbornly defending their position.

The world is rife with hostilities that refuse to heal: everything from family squabbles, church splits, labor/management disagreements, to hostage situations, racial confrontations, and international conflicts. And when two sides deadlock over an issue, the need for an arbitrator becomes essential.

An arbitrator is also known as a go-between or a liaison. In the Scriptures, the term used to describe this important role is *mediator*. And the One who mediated reconciliation in the most profound and vast rift—that between God and sinful humanity—is Christ, our Mediator.

Mediator: The Word Itself

To begin our study of this wonderful word, let's do a little excavating to uncover its meaning, past and present.

Its Meaning Then and Now

In first-century Greece, the word for *mediator* was *mesitēs*, which came from the root word *mesos*, meaning "in the middle." Quite literally, a *mesitēs* was a middleman, someone who worked to settle differences and bring about a peaceful reconciliation between two opposing sides.

Today the function of a mediator is much the same. One familiar example would be an umpire in a baseball game. It's that person's

job to mediate between two opposing teams who are prone to dis-
agree over what's fair or foul, safe or out, ball or strike. Without
such a mediator, it's doubtful any baseball game would ever reach
the bottom of the ninth.

Its Appearances in Scripture

In the Greek version of the Old Testament, the only place we
find the word *mesitēs* is in Job 9. And, interestingly enough, it's
translated "umpire."

As you may recall, Job was a righteous man whose ten children
were killed, whose servants were slain, and whose livestock was
either stolen or burned in a whirlwind of catastrophes. In addition,
Satan afflicted him with agonizing open ulcers that made his life
worse than miserable. In the midst of his suffering, Job concluded
that God must unfairly think him a wicked man to assault him with
such calamities, and he lamented,

> "For He is not a man as I am that I may answer Him,
> That we may go to court together.
> There is no umpire between us,
> Who may lay his hand upon us both."
> (vv. 32–33)

Job longed for a *mesitēs*, someone who would act as a middleman
between heaven and earth, to bring God and him together to settle
their differences and end his suffering.

Moving from the Old Testament to the New, we find this same
term in Galatians 3:20a: "Now a mediator is not for one party only."

Unlike the role of an advocate, who pleads the cause of one
side, a mediator seeks to fairly represent both parties.

And in 1 Timothy 2, the apostle Paul not only identifies Christ
as the Mediator, but also clearly names the two parties He fairly
represents.

> For there is one God, and one mediator also between
> God and men, the man Christ Jesus. (v. 2:5)

Its Theological and Practical Importance

To fully appreciate Christ's role as our mediator, we must first
understand the problem that separates us from God: sin. Because
of our unrighteousness and disobedience, an eternal chasm exists
that separates us from the Lord, who is holy, pure, and righteous
(Isa. 59:1–2).

Without the help of a mediator, all humankind would be hopelessly deadlocked as enemies of God, doomed to an eternity in hell. But God sent His only Son, Jesus, to mediate the situation. By becoming a man—the only sinless person who ever lived—Christ brought humanity and divinity together. But the chasm between us and the Father was not actually bridged until "He made Him who knew no sin to be sin on our behalf" (2 Cor. 5:21a). It was while Christ hung on a cross, suspended between sinful humanity and His holy Father, that our sins were paid for by His blood and the chasm was crossed.

With his usual keen insight and sensitivity, William Barclay explains how Jesus fulfilled three essential qualities of a mediator.

> (i) The *mesitēs* must be able perfectly to represent both parties in the dispute. He must fully understand and sympathise with both. Otherwise his decision is bound to be prejudiced, one-sided, unjust and inequitable. Jesus is therefore the only possible mediator between God and man, because he is perfectly God and man. . . .
>
> (ii) The first duty of the mediator is to establish communication between the two parties who are in dispute. In the case of Jesus the problem was not to establish communication between God and man, for God never needed to be reconciled to man; the problem was to establish communication between man and God. . . .
>
> (iii) But the task of the mediator goes beyond merely establishing communication; he has to establish between the two conflicting parties a new relationship in which suspicion has turned to trust, enmity to friendship, and hatred to love. There lies the heart of the matter. It was the essential task of the mediator to establish, not merely a legal relationship, but a personal relationship in which love is the bond. Jesus is not the mediator who brings two legal disputants together; he is the mediator who brings together two lovers who have drifted apart and for whom life can never be complete until they are in fellowship again.[1]

1. William Barclay, *Jesus as They Saw Him* (1962; reprint, Grand Rapids, Mich.: William B. Eerdmans Publishing Co., 1980), pp. 337–38.

Key Usages in the New Testament

Let's turn now to the key New Testament texts about our Mediator.

1 Timothy 2:1–6

We've already looked at verse 5 for the identities of the Mediator and the two parties in conflict. But when we examine the context around this verse, we'll discover a telling truth about the nature of the chasm between us.

> First of all, then, I urge that entreaties and prayers, petitions and thanksgivings, be made on behalf of all men, for kings and all who are in authority, in order that we may lead a tranquil and quiet life in all godliness and dignity. This is good and acceptable in the sight of God our Savior, who desires all men to be saved and to come to the knowledge of the truth. For there is one God, and one mediator also between God and men, the man Christ Jesus, who gave Himself as a ransom for all, the testimony borne at the proper time. (vv. 1–6)

As Paul clearly states, the Lord God "desires all men to be saved and to come to the knowledge of the truth." So the problem that has caused a chasm between us and God is not with Him but with our own sinful rebelliousness. We're the ones who rejected God, not the other way around. We created the need for a mediator to bring us back together again.

Hebrews 8:1–7

Throughout Hebrews, the superiority of Christ is expounded again and again. He is presented as superior to humankind, the angels, the Law, and, here in chapter 8, the Old Testament high priests.

> Now the main point in what has been said is this: we have such a high priest, who has taken His seat at the right hand of the throne of the Majesty in the heavens, a minister in the sanctuary, and in the true tabernacle, which the Lord pitched, not man. For every high priest is appointed to offer both gifts and sacrifices; hence it is necessary that this high priest also have something to offer. Now if He

were on earth, He would not be a priest at all, since there are those who offer the gifts according to the Law; who serve a copy and shadow of the heavenly things. . . . But now He has obtained a more excellent ministry, by as much as He is also the mediator of a better covenant, which has been enacted on better promises. For if that first covenant had been faultless, there would have been no occasion sought for a second. (vv. 1–7)

In the old covenant that God established with Israel, it was the sole privilege and responsibility of the high priest to enter the Holy of Holies once a year. This was a place inside the tabernacle where God's presence resided, and here the high priest would offer a sacrifice as an atonement for all the people's sins (see Lev. 16).

When Jesus came, however, He established a new covenant by offering up the superior sacrifice of Himself as an atonement for our sins. And in doing so, He serves as our High Priest to mediate a "better covenant," one where we each, through faith in Him, can enter into a face-to-face relationship with the living God.

Hebrews 9:11–15

Jesus is pictured as the mediator of a new covenant again in Hebrews 9, only this time the emphasis is more on the superiority of Christ's blood, which was shed—once for all—for the forgiveness of sins.

But when Christ appeared as a high priest of the good things to come, He entered through the greater and more perfect tabernacle, not made with hands, that is to say, not of this creation; and not through the blood of goats and calves, but through His own blood, He entered the holy place once for all, having obtained eternal redemption. For if the blood of goats and bulls and the ashes of a heifer sprinkling those who have been defiled, sanctify for the cleansing of the flesh, how much more will the blood of Christ, who through the eternal Spirit offered Himself without blemish to God, cleanse your conscience from dead works to serve the living God? And for this reason He is the mediator of a new covenant, in order that since a death has taken place for the redemption of the transgressions that were committed under the first covenant, those who have been called may receive the promise of the eternal inheritance. (vv. 11–15)

When the high priest entered the Holy of Holies inside the tabernacle on the Day of Atonement, he would sprinkle the blood of a sacrificial bull and goat on the mercy seat and thus procure forgiveness for the people's sins that year. However, through Jesus' precious blood, which was sprinkled on the new covenant's mercy seat of the cross, we have eternal redemption. This means that we don't have to rely on the blood of sacrificed animals to please God. Jesus' blood has secured for us reconciliation for eternity.

Hebrews 12:18–24

In our final passage, notice the thought progression. The writer begins by telling us about something we *haven't* come to and ends by telling us what we *have* come to.

> For you have not come to a mountain that may be touched and to a blazing fire, and to darkness and gloom and whirlwind, and to the blast of a trumpet and the sound of words which sound was such that those who heard begged that no further word should be spoken to them. For they could not bear the command, "If even a beast touches the mountain, it will be stoned." And so terrible was the sight, that Moses said, "I am full of fear and trembling." But you have come to Mount Zion and to the city of the living God, the heavenly Jerusalem, and to myriads of angels, to the general assembly and church of the first-born who are enrolled in heaven, and to God, the Judge of all, and to the spirits of righteous men made perfect, and to Jesus, the mediator of a new covenant, and to the sprinkled blood, which speaks better than the blood of Abel. (vv. 18–24)

Did you detect three important mountains in this passage? First, the author vividly recalls the darkness, gloom, and fearful nature of Mount Sinai, where Israel received the old covenant (v. 18; see also Exod. 19–20). The people were so afraid to hear God's voice that they begged Moses to be God's messenger to them.

In contrast to that unapproachable mountain is a second, Mount Zion, which represents the new covenant achieved by Jesus, our Mediator (Heb. 12:22–23). Through His blood shed on a third mount, Mount Calvary, He "took away the terror of Mount Sinai and gave to men the glory of the new relationship with God; it was Jesus, the perfect priest and the perfect sacrifice, who made the unapproachable approachable."[2]

Reasons We Are Grateful for a Mediator

From our study, at least three reasons can be given for why we should be thankful for Jesus as our Mediator. First, He has brought reconciliation where there once was alienation. Second, He has bridged the distance that once separated us from God. And third, He has become our peace.

> Therefore having been justified by faith, we have peace with God through our Lord Jesus Christ. . . . God demonstrates His own love toward us, in that while we were yet sinners, Christ died for us. Much more then, having now been justified by His blood, we shall be saved from the wrath of God through Him. For if while we were enemies, we were reconciled to God through the death of His Son, much more, having been reconciled, we shall be saved by His life. (Rom. 5:1, 8–10)

◆

Dear Father,
Thank You for sending Jesus, the magnificent Mediator who bridged the gap, who replaced the old covenant with the new, who reconciled me to You because of Your great love for me.
Thank You, Jesus, for bringing us together at the cost of Your own precious blood. You have brought amity where there was only enmity, joy where there was only sorrow, hope where there was only despair.
Such a love, such a sacrifice. May I love and give of myself sacrificially so that others might come to have peace with You as You have given me. Amen.

2. William Barclay, *The Letter to the Hebrews,* 2d ed., The Daily Study Bible Series (Philadelphia, Pa.: Westminster Press, 1957), pp. 213–14.

Have you ever run across these verses from 2 Corinthians?

> God, who reconciled us to Himself through Christ . . .
> gave us the ministry of reconciliation. . . .
>   Therefore, we are ambassadors for Christ, as
> though God were entreating through us.
> (2 Cor. 5:18b, 20a)

Once we are reconciled, we in turn become reconcilers. Are you fulfilling this ministry God has entrusted to you?

Thinking back to the essential qualities of a mediator that William Barclay outlined for us, answer the following questions, keeping in mind an unsaved friend.

First, how well are you representing both parties? Do you understand your friend's feelings and questions? Are you sympathetic, patient, willing to listen? And how well do you convey God's views?

_____

_____

_____

Second, how solid is your basis of communication with this person? Are you cultivating a genuine friendship based on openness and honesty? In what ways are you opening the lines of communication between your friend and your Savior?

_____

_____

_____

Third, in what specific ways is your relationship helping your friend replace suspicion of Christ with trust, enmity with friendship, hatred with love?

_____

_____

_____

Take some time now to worship your Mediator with a grateful heart, letting the following statements focus you.

- *He has brought reconciliation where there once was alienation.* Allow yourself to remember what it was like before you met Christ, when you were alienated from God. Now give Him heartfelt thanks for bringing you to Himself through faith in His Son.

- *He has bridged the distance that once separated us from God.* Remember that lonely night in the Garden of Gethsemane, when Jesus agonized over the horror of paying the penalty of your sins. Remember that dark, friendless hour when He was arrested. Remember when He was beaten and whipped, spit upon and crucified. Remember when He bore the full weight of your sins and His blood was shed for your forgiveness. Thank Him for obeying the Father, for going to the cross on your behalf, like a lamb to the shearer.

- *He has become our peace.* Bathe yourself in the wonderful news that you have peace with God through Jesus. No longer distant and at enmity with you, God is now your loving Father.

Journal

_____

_____

_____

_____

_____

_____

_____

_____

Chapter 12

WE HAVE AN ADVOCATE
1 John 2:1–2

"My name is a gift which I offer to you."[1]

Just the mention of certain names has a way of bringing comfort. Perhaps for you it is the name of your father or mother, a grandparent or friend or spouse. You speak that individual's name and a deep sense of joy resonates in your heart. Why? Because that name belongs to someone who loves you, someone you can count on, someone who will be there when you need them, no matter what. It's a name that anchors you, gives you stability, provides constancy in a constantly changing world.

Such treasured names are becoming rare in our materialistic, fragmented, selfish society. We have our cars, clothes, and condos, but we have no names.

In this, our final lesson, Jesus offers us the gift of another priceless name. He has already given us thirteen wonderful titles that have a powerful way of bringing comfort. But once we unwrap this last title, become intimately acquainted with its meaning, learn to speak it; we will possess the cherished name of Someone we can count on, Someone who will be there when we need Him—no matter what.

Who would that Someone be? His name is Advocate.

The Meaning and Importance of an Advocate

To understand the significance of this title, let's conduct a brief background study of its use in our everyday world and in the Scriptures.

In the World

According to *Webster's*, an advocate is "one that pleads the cause of another."[2] Perhaps the most familiar example of this is seen in a court of law, where attorneys act as advocates for either the prosecution or the defense. But even in ancient Greece, an

---

1. Madeleine L'Engle, *Walking on Water: Reflections on Faith and Art* (Wheaton, Ill.: Harold Shaw Publishers, 1980), p. 111.

2. *Webster's Ninth New Collegiate Dictionary*, see "advocate."

advocate was someone who counseled, coached, and championed the cause of another in court.

> The [advocate] was the friend of the accused person, called in to speak in support of his character, in order to enlist the sympathy of the judges in his favour. . . . It means someone who will present someone else's case to some other person or to some other authority in the most favorable light.[3]

In the Scriptures

The New Testament Greek word for advocate is made of two terms, *para*, meaning "alongside," and *kaleo*, which means "to call." Combined, *parakletos* conveys the idea of one called alongside to assist, defend, or intercede on behalf of another.

Interestingly, the only writer in all of Scripture to use this term is the apostle John. In his gospel, *parakletos* is repeatedly mentioned in the Upper Room Discourse (John 13–17), and in each case it refers to the Holy Spirit. Let's briefly examine this passage for what it reveals about the role of an advocate, beginning in John 14.

To put what we're about to read into context, remember that Christ and the disciples were celebrating Passover on what was to be their last night together. Jesus knew that there was precious little time left before He would be arrested, tried, and crucified. He also knew that His disciples would be left behind, lonely and afraid. So He offered them the assurance of One who would come to them in His place.

> "And I will ask the Father, and He will give you another Helper, that He may be with you forever."
> (v. 16)

The Greek term for *helper* is the same word from which we get *advocate*. Here, and in several other passages, Jesus uses this term in reference to the Holy Spirit. It is this third member of the Trinity who would come alongside the disciples and be their constant companion, their *parakletos*. In the King James Version of this passage, the word used to describe the Holy Spirit is "Comforter." And in

---

3. William Barclay, *More New Testament Words* (New York, N.Y.: Harper and Brothers Publishers, 1958), pp. 131–32.

the New International Version, He is called the "Counselor." All of them fit. The Spirit of God comes alongside to help, comfort, and to counsel.

Later in this same discourse, Jesus expanded on the role of the Helper, saying that He would "teach you all things, and bring to your remembrance all that I said to you"; that He would "bear witness of Me" and "convict the world concerning sin, and righteousness, and judgment" (v. 26; 15:26; 16:8; see also 6:9–11).

So far, all these references describe the Holy Spirit. But if we turn from John's gospel to his first epistle, we find the only passage in all the Bible where Christ is called our Advocate.

Thirty years had passed since that night in the Upper Room. During that time, John had pondered deeply on the miracles and teachings he'd seen and heard as a disciple; and having reflected on these, he put his thoughts down in a letter written with the tenderness of a grandfather to his children.

> My little children, I am writing these things to you that you may not sin. And if anyone sins, we have an Advocate with the Father, Jesus Christ the righteous; and He Himself is the propitiation for our sins; and not for ours only, but also for those of the whole world. (1 John 2:1–2)

The Theology and Practicality of Our Advocate

With all that we've learned thus far about the role of an advocate, let's get acquainted with Jesus Christ the righteous, our Advocate with the Father.

What It Means

John sincerely desired that we not sin, but if we do, we have a defense attorney, Jesus, who will represent us before the throne of God. Commentator Kenneth Wuest sheds some light on the way Jesus might plead our case.

> Our Advocate does not plead that we are innocent or adduce extenuating circumstances. He acknowledges our guilt and presents His vicarious work as the ground of our acquital. He stands in the Court of Heaven *a Lamb as it had been slain* (Rev. 5:6), and the marks of His sore passion are a mute but eloquent

appeal: "I suffered all this for sinners, and shall it go for naught?"[4]

Only Jesus is qualified to make such an appeal, for only He has satisfied all the righteous requirements of the Father.

John also reveals something important when he tells us that we have an Advocate "with the Father." That little word *with* means that Jesus stands face-to-face with the Father. He doesn't plead our cause through assistant angels; He Himself goes before the Father and makes petitions on our behalf. A. T. Robertson made the observation:

> The Holy Spirit is God's Advocate on earth with men, while Christ is man's Advocate with the Father.[5]

Why It's Essential

All of us have a need for Jesus to be our Advocate for several reasons. *First,* we need an Advocate because we continue to sin and continuously need forgiveness and fellowship. In contrast to God, whom John describes as "light, and in Him there is no darkness at all" (1 John 1:5), we are all shown by Paul to be sinners who would not seek God if He weren't already seeking us (see Rom. 3:10–11, 23). When you hold our sinfulness up against the pure light of God's holiness, it's easy to see why we need an Advocate.

Second, an Advocate is necessary because we are weak and need extra strength to press on. In Hebrews we're told that Jesus sympathizes with our weaknesses and continually intercedes on our behalf so that "we may receive mercy and may find grace to help in time of need" (4:16; see also vv. 14–15; 7:25).

Third, we need an Advocate with the Father because we are constantly being accused. In Revelation 12:10, Satan is pictured as the "accuser of our brethren." Like a ruthless prosecuting attorney, he brings accusations against us "before our God day and night." Satan wants to put us away in that prison he himself will one day be locked in forever—hell. And he would win every case hands down if our Advocate wasn't there to show He's already paid the penalty for our sins.

4. Kenneth S. Wuest, *In These Last Days* (Grand Rapids, Mich.: William B. Eerdmans Publishing Co., 1954), p. 109.

5. A. T. Robertson, *Word Pictures in the New Testament* (Nashville, Tenn.: Broadman Press, 1933), vol. 6, p. 209.

Some of the Lasting Benefits

As with other treasured names, the mention of Jesus' name Advocate has a way of bringing comfort. It's a name that anchors us, gives us stability, provides constancy, and holds forth the hope of the following lasting benefits:

- *We have been justified before God.* Justification is the sovereign act of God whereby He declares righteous the believing sinners while we are still in a sinning state. That's grace, and that's what the Advocate procures for us.

- *We claim forgiveness for our sins.* Through Christ's advocacy, we are continually washed clean in the eyes of God.

- *We gain strength in the midst of our own weakness.* Jesus knows our frailties; He has suffered our infirmities and is able to strengthen us in our need.

- *We live confidently in spite of the adversary's accusations.* Satan's implacable hostility and relentless barrage of accusations against us are constantly being frustrated and thrown out of God's court because of Christ our Advocate!

◆

Dear Advocate,
  No one knows me like You do. Every day You stand before the throne of God to defend me in all my sinfulness. Still, You love me; You never tire from counseling, comforting, helping me. Thank You for the wonderful gift of being my Advocate, for removing my guilt each time Satan accuses me before God. Your name truly is wonderful! Amen.

Living Insights

In his comprehensive work *All the Divine Names and Titles in the Bible,* author Herbert Lockyer draws an interesting comparison between the "work of an earthly advocate" and the "unceasing advocacy of Jesus in Heaven."

> 1. [An earthly advocate] must be a wise and learned person in the court of judicature—this our heavenly Advocate is (Colossians 2:3).

2. He must belong to the Law, which is the rule for him in practice. Christ satisfied the Law for us by His death (Galatians 3:13; 4:4), and likewise fulfilled the Law for us by His obedience (Romans 5:19).

3. He must have the Judge's ear more than others, having full authority to speak, which Jesus has (John 11:42). The ground of His pleading is Calvary, which gives Him all-prevailing power with the Judge of all the earth.

4. He must be careful to keep up the honor of the Judge, to prevent any contempt of Court. In His high-priestly prayer of John 17, our heavenly Advocate illustrated this feature.[6]

Following Lockyer's lead, brainstorm a few comparisons of your own between earthly advocates and our heavenly Advocate.

_____

_____

_____

🍇 *Living Insights*   STUDY TWO

Oftentimes in our worship, we make the mistake of praising Jesus solely for what He can do for us, rather than for who He is. Such a one-sided understanding of worship transforms our love into selfishness, with the focus really on ourselves.

So to close our time of worship for the entire guide, let's instead praise Jesus for who He has revealed Himself to be in each of His titles. Beside the names listed below, write down at least one word that best describes the attribute you associate with that name. Then let this be your starting point in praising Him.

Lord _____

King of Kings, Lord of Lords _____

6. Herbert Lockyer, *All the Divine Names and Titles in the Bible* (Grand Rapids, Mich.: Zondervan Publishing House, Lamplighter Books, 1975), p. 109.

Messiah _____

The Alpha and the Omega _____

Mighty King _____

Suffering Servant _____

Ideal Man _____

Divine Son _____

The True Vine _____

The Shepherd of the Sheep _____

The Lamb of God _____

The Way, the Truth, the Life _____

Mediator _____

Advocate _____

Journal

_____

_____

_____

_____

_____

_____

_____

_____

_____

_____

_____

BOOKS FOR PROBING FURTHER

To learn more about the Savior through His names, we recommend the following books.

Barclay, William. *Jesus as They Saw Him*. 1962. Reprint. Grand Rapids, Mich.: William B. Eerdmans Publishing Co., 1980.

Gariepy, Henry. *100 Portraits of Christ*. Wheaton, Ill.: Scripture Press Publications, Victor Books, 1993.

Keller, W. Phillip. *A Layman Looks at the Lamb of God*. Minneapolis, Minn.: Bethany House Publishers, 1982.

———. *A Shepherd Looks at the Good Shepherd and His Sheep*. Grand Rapids, Mich.: Zondervan Publishing House, Daybreak Books, 1978.

Lockyer, Herbert. *All the Divine Names and Titles in the Bible*. Grand Rapids, Mich.: Zondervan Publishing House, Lamplighter Books, 1975.

Loeks, Mary Foxwell. *The Glorious Names of God*. Grand Rapids, Mich.: Baker Book House, 1986.

Powell, Ivor. *Bible Names of Christ*. Grand Rapids, Mich.: Kregel Publications, 1988.

Rolls, Charles J. *The Names and Titles of Jesus Christ*. 5 vols. Neptune, N.J.: Loizeaux, 1984–86.

Spurgeon, Charles H. *C. H. Spurgeon's Sermons on Christ's Names and Titles*. Edited by Charles T. Cook. 1961. Reprint. Greenwood, S.C.: Attic Press, 1965.

Some of the books listed may be out of print and available only through a library. For those currently available, please contact your local Christian bookstore. Books by Charles R. Swindoll may be obtained through Insight for Living, as well as some books by other authors. Just call the IFL office that serves you.

ACKNOWLEDGMENTS

Insight for Living is grateful to the sources listed below for permission to use their material.

Barclay, William. *Jesus as They Saw Him.* London, England: SCM Press, 1962. Reprint. Grand Rapids, Mich.: William B. Eerdmans Publishing Co., 1980.

Levitt, Zola. *The Miracle of Passover.* Dallas, Tex.: Zola Levitt, 1977. (See Zola Levitt Ministries, Box 12268, Dallas, Texas 75225.)

Lucado, Max. *No Wonder They Call Him the Savior.* Portland, Oreg.: Multomah Press, 1986.

NOTES

NOTES

NOTES

NOTES

ORDERING INFORMATION

HIS NAME IS WONDERFUL

If you would like to order additional study guides, purchase the cassette series that accompanies this guide, or request our product catalogs, please contact the office that serves you.

United States and International locations:

Insight for Living
Post Office Box 69000
Anaheim, CA 92817-0900

1-800-772-8888, 24 hours a day, 7 days a week
(714) 575-5000, 8:00 A.M. to 4:30 P.M., Pacific time, Monday to Friday

Canada:

Insight for Living Ministries
Post Office Box 2510
Vancouver, BC, Canada V6B 3W7

1-800-663-7639, 24 hours a day, 7 days a week

Australia:

Insight for Living, Inc.
General Post Office Box 2823 EE
Melbourne, VIC 3001, Australia

(03) 9877-4277, 8:30 A.M. to 5:00 P.M., Monday to Friday

World Wide Web:

www.insight.org

Study Guide Subscription Program

Study guide subscriptions are available. Please call or write the office nearest you to find out how you can receive our study guides on a regular basis.